RAILROADED IN HARRIS COUNTY

Dell Robinson

RAILROADED IN HARRIS COUNTY

ISBN-13: 978-1461026457
ISBN-10: 1461026458

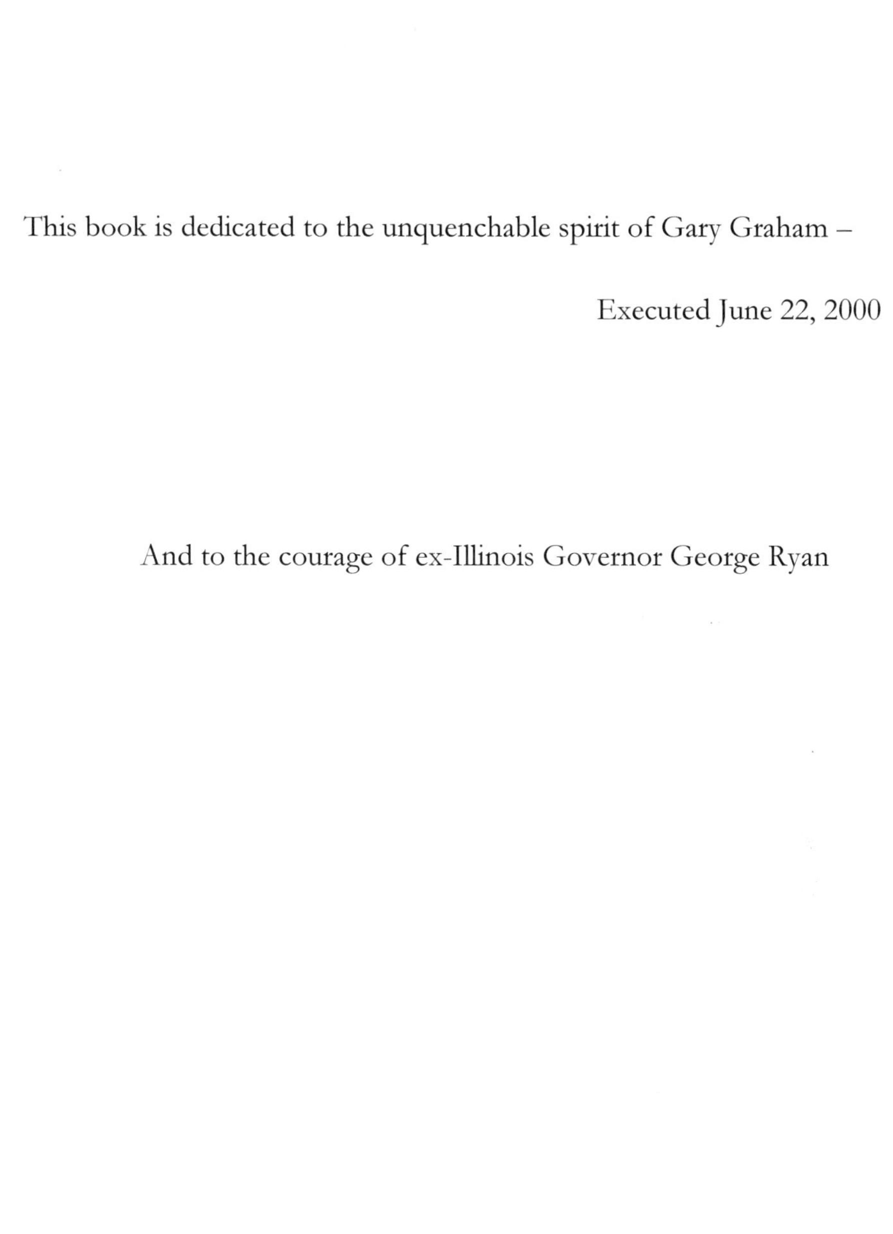

This book is dedicated to the unquenchable spirit of Gary Graham –

Executed June 22, 2000

And to the courage of ex-Illinois Governor George Ryan

I know why the caged bird beats his wings.

It is not a carol of joy or glee,

But a prayer that he sends from his heart's

Deep cove, But a plea, that upward to heaven

He flings –

I know why the cage bird sings!

Paul Laurence Dunbar

Introduction

What causes wrongful convictions? In response to this question one is likely to receive a variety of answers depending on who is asked and where they fall on the ideological spectrum.

For the honest hardworking people within the Criminal Justice system-- judges, prosecutors, detectives -- wrongful convictions are isolated events, anomalies that so rarely occur they need not be given much consideration.

But for innocent men and women who spend decades, or more languishing in prisons around the nation fighting a David vs Goliath battle to prove their innocence, their families who bare the stigma of incarceration along with them and the defense attorneys who work tirelessly to free them on shoe-string budgets, wrongful convictions are more than isolated events. Any time an innocent person is sent to prison, it represents a systematic breakdown of the system; a system that has put an increasing emphasis on winning convictions and retribution at the expense of truth and justice.

And while there may be little consensus on what causes wrongful convictions that they occur and at a alarming rate is no longer in dispute, the 250 DNA exonerations over the last decade having proved as much. The who of wrongful convictions is equally far from mysterious with poor racial minorities bearing the brunt of the injustice?

However, with less than three-hundred people proven innocent by DNA in the last decade out of a prison population of over two million, 156,000 in Texas alone, the question must be asked, and at some point seriously answered: How many more innocent men and women are trapped in prisons around the nation unheard and unheralded; their cries and pleas continuously falling on death ears. Yet in a system of such magnitude what should be considered an acceptable rate of wrongful convictions?

According to New York District Judge John Collins:

"The greatest crime of all in a civilized society is a unjust conviction. It is truly a scandal which reflects unfavorably on all participants in the criminal justice system."

Is this really so? Or are unjust convictions simply the cost of doing business when fallible humans set in judgment of other fallible humans?

In telling the story of one young man's decade and a half quest to free himself from a wrongful conviction, "Railroaded In Harris County," attempts to answer some of these fundamental questions?

Contents

Chapter One - Voire Dire

"It shall be the primary duty of all prosecuting attorneys...not to convict, but to ensure that justice is done"

Texas Code of Criminal Procedure Article 2.01

In a new dark grey suit that fit well on his slim frame, standing before 50 to 60 potential jurors assembled in the acting 176 District Courtroom[1], across the street from the regular courthouse at 1201 Franklin the prosecutor Steve Baldassano begin outlining the state's case by running the jury pool through various run-of-the mill scenarios that might potentially apply to the case at hand.

First was the issue of alcohol intoxication or drug abuse and how neither could constitute a defense to a crime in Texas. He told the jury pool, "Let me go through some of the things that possibly could be involved in this case and some of the laws in Texas that apply.

Let's try one--voluntarily intoxication. It's not a defense to a crime if you're voluntarily intoxicated. That is, you can't get all liquored up and then go and shoot your boss, and then say, "Hey, I was drunk."

---

1. The West case was originally assigned to the 176th District Court where the elected judge was the Honorable Brian Rains. However due to a scheduling conflict with the high profile Capital Murder trial of Robert Angleton, West's trial was transferred to a "project court, "overseen by visiting judge Robert C. Burdette. Visiting judges are retired judges, or judges who have lost their seats in previous elections. Commenting on this system veteran defense .attorney David A. Jones said, "The institution has its own standards, as it applies to Burdette, it's called speed in all things. Dispose of cases/dispose of people, and you're okay with them."

Assuming his point was made he was about to move on when a juror objected. After raising his hand the man said, "I personally had some experience, something in the past. I did suffer that. I had some black-outs."

Baldassano gave the man a quick legal answer that satisfied him and then dove into his next point, a point more relevant to the State's case in the instant trial.

The prosecutor was about to try a case where the only evidence came from questionable witnesses, convicted felons, as well as friends of the victim who waited months to talk to detectives involved in the case casting doubt on the truthfulness and accuracy of their testimony.

With the I.D issue being the pink elephant in the room, Baldassano had to get it out in the open and dealt with. If he didn't, the case of West vs. Texas would be over before it ever began.

Taking the initiative on the credibility issue, he called on a juror, "Miss Riggins, how would you assess the credibility of a witness or anybody?"

"What they say."

Most people would consider Baldassano handsome with his curly hair and dark features; he had a certain boyish charm that he seemed to be able to cut on and off at will. He looked around the small courtroom at the early morning faces staring back at him and took a informal poll of the heads that nodded at Miss Riggins common sense answer. Good, but not good enough. He needed more clarification. Common sense might not guarantee a conviction. He said, "Okay, everybody basically agrees with that? You might look and see what the witness said, if it makes sense, how it fit with what another witness says. You might look at how it fits with physical evidence at the scene. You might listen to how the witness is testifying. Whether they have prior convictions or have been to prison before. You might consider that for whatever you want."

He had said it. It was out in the open. In so many words, he was telling the potential jurors my witnesses might be shady, have questionable backgrounds, contradicting stories, but remember we already told you that, not the defense. The state's not trying to hide anything. Furthermore, none of that matters.

To be sure, he waited; when no one said anything, he was elated. Things were going better than expected, which wasn't always the case. Sometimes the potential jurors were so contentious the entire jury pool had to be shuffled.

Not this morning.

"Let me talk to you a little bit about description versus recognition. Would everybody agree with me that it's easier to recognize somebody then to describe them?"

Right here the prosecutor was on a slippery slope and sought to make his point by calling on various jurors and asking them to describe the bailiff that escorted them into the courtroom that morning.

A few jurors were able to describe the man and a couple others, not very enthusiastic about being called upon to perform their civic duty, had outright ignored him.

What the prosecutor was actually inquiring about had more to do with attention than description vs. recognition. It was a scientific fact that before something or someone could be adequately recalled, a certain amount of attention had to be paid to the initial phenomenon, generally the more the better.

Majority of the potential jurors assembled that morning could've cared less what the bailiff looked like; therefore, they never paid the man any attention to begin with. But without anyone present in the courtroom to challenge his erroneous assertion, fiction became fact as often happens in courtrooms around the nation. The truth was reduced down to mere appearance.

Baldassano sought to capitalize on the jurors' inattention, "Can everybody agree it's a lot easier to recognize him than it might have been to describe him?"

A female juror verbally agreed.

Don Irvin, the defense attorney for the 20 year old defendant, sat in pensive silence as he listened to the prosecutor's attempt to immunize the jury pool to every weakness in the state's case. So far, he had managed to put before the jurors that voluntarily intoxication wasn't a defense; that the state's case rested on the word of convicted felons and individuals of questionable character; and that because a witness couldn't describe a person they saw, it didn't necessarily mean they didn't see them.

With the defendant and his attorney looking on, the prosecutor turned up the voltage on his thousand watt smile and said, "Okay, let me talk to you about one witness testimony. In the State of Texas, the State can legally prove a case using one witness.

I would like to have 50,000 witnesses.[2] But, the law says that if the jury believes the evidence of a person's guilt beyond a reasonable doubt, and there's only one witness, you can convict."

Baldassano had received his law degree at South Texas College of Law, one of the better programs in the State. Such training had served him well in his chosen profession. He paused to make eye contact with each and every potential juror. Twelve would sit in judgment of their hypothetical peer. Notwithstanding the fact that few of the 50 to 60 men and women assembled in the 176th District Courtroom, many from Houston's better zip codes had very little if anything in common with the 20 year old unemployed African American whose fate they would decide. Like a lot of aspects of the legal profession, "Jury of peers," was nothing more than legal jargon left over from the days of English Common law. The word didn't mean what the defendant, or most lay people thought it did.

His last point concerning the number of witnesses was crucial to the case and he had to be sure, "Does anybody have a problem finding anybody guilty based on the evidence of Just one witness?

Would anybody have a problem finding somebody guilty? Raise your hand if you could not?" He was taking no chances; without a pro-prosecution convict a dead man jury, it would be impossible for the state to win a conviction; the evidence was too thin.

---

2. While not quite 50,000 it would seem that in the instant case the prosecutor would at least be able to produce a few hundred. Considering there were 1,500 potential witnesses.

A juror raised her hand, "There's just some doubt there. It would have to be beyond a shadow of a doubt, not a shadow, but very convincing, if you're talking about a murder charge."

Baldassano faced the juror, "Okay could you do it, if the person convinced you, or could it be that just nobody could convince you?"

That juror daring to be honest about her feelings opened a flood gate, soon several more hands popped up. Meticulously he noted and scratched them from the pool of potential jurors. They were all wrong for the jury; they showed an inclination to question and to act on those questions. Jurors like that were likely to acquit an innocent man.

He turned to the indictment, "Does everybody understand the indictment? You'll notice some things not in there; for example, motive. We don't have to prove motive. That could be something you're interested in, but it's nothing we have to prove beyond a reasonable doubt?"

Immediately it was clear many of the jurors didn't agree."Wait a minute," looks jumped from one face to the next. A minor revolt of conscious seemed to be taking place and the potential jurors appeared to be saying, "You're asking for too much. Don't bring one or two un-creditable witnesses in here who aren't sure what they saw, or who they saw and tell me this young man killed someone for no apparent reason, at least not one that you have to prove. Wait just one minute."

Baldassano saw this ideological shift and tried to regain control, "Mr. Ray how do you feel about that? You can see that, that's not in the indictment, first of all?"

Mr. Ray, "A motive?"

"Right."

"Yes, I could if it's not in the indictment. It seems to me it would be a central part of the case."

Employing hyperbole the prosecutor conjured up an outrageous scenario about a random shooting to try and make his point. When he finished, he turned back to the intelligent juror who expressed what others in the room were likely thinking themselves, that people don't usually kill people without a reason.

Being conflict-shy, a few jurors squirmed in their seats under Baldassano's piercing glare thankful they weren't the target of the prosecutor's ire.

Chastened, Mr. Ray was now on board, "I understand." Still, the veteran prosecutor scanned the faces of the other jurors, sought consensus, "Does everybody agree with that; that we don't have to prove motive? Because that's not something in the indictment?"

This time, around the room was silent the jurors appeared to be holding their breath while the prosecutor made his final point.

"Also that a gun was found, or any type of physical evidence, we don't have to prove."

When the court recessed for the day, Baldassano had systematically walked the jury pool through every weakness in the state's case. Essentially telling the jury, hey this is a weak case; don't expect a lot. But that doesn't matter.

Such a disclaimer served two purposes. First, it prevented the jurors from retiring to the jury room and saying, "Is that all?" And second, it assured the seating of a certain kind of jury; a jury that wouldn't concern itself with the credibility of witnesses, or a lack of witnesses; with why the person was killed; or why the state didn't have one piece of physical evidence connecting the defendant to the crime. In short, the prosecutor sought and seated a jury that would convict an innocent man.

Chapter Two - The Trial

> *"A jury is charged with deciding matters of fact and Dellivering a verdict of guilt or innocence based on the evidence."*
>
> -- West's Encyclopedia of American Law

The defendant was charged with killing 23 year old Efrem Breaux and 25 year old Sammie Ray Johnson. The first case the prosecutor wanted to try him for was the death of 25 year old Sammie Ray Johnson because West professed zero involvement in Mr. Johnson's death for the longest the case had been little more than an afterthought for him.

From the moment the homicide detectives investigating the case approached him up until the start of his trial, he had seen it as little more than a shysty tactic of the prosecution to either get him to cop-out or to squeeze him for information they believed he had. Such tactics often referred to as over-charging weren't entirely unheard of, but in his mind, he hadn't done anything, therefore he didn't have anything to worry about; they couldn't convict him for something he didn't do.

It wasn't until one of the detectives told him that two witnesses had allegedly identified him as one of the shooters that he tried to recollect what he remembered about the night of June 6, 1997, which wasn't much, but it was enough for him to know that these two witnesses were either mistaken or they were outright lying.

The more he thought about it, his memory of the night actually begin three days earlier the night his girlfriend Stephanie gave birth to his twin daughters. For West they were his first kids and he was overjoyed.

On the night of June 6, 1997 he left Stephanie's apartment on his way home. Her apartment was a block from the Carrington club on South Main. He pulled up to the stop sign of Westgate.

From South Main all the way back to the Astrodome he saw one big traffic jam and wondered what was going on. Cutting the radio on 97.9 The Box, a local Hip-Hop station, was broadcasting from the just ended Boxapolooza concert which had featured Lil Kim and several other rappers. With the concert over the DJ was inviting everyone to the after-party at the Carrington's club.

A red flag went up in his mind. A year earlier the Carrington club had been one of his favorite haunts. But several months earlier a incident across the street at the Exxon station had changed that. And he had vowed his nightclub days were over. Alcohol, attitudes and raging hormones didn't mix. And because his own father wasn't in his life he wanted to be there for his daughters, to do so he had to stay out of jail and alive.

These thoughts were running through his mind as he watched the traffic in front of him on Westgate. So while he had a thousand reason not to go he ignored them all and instead of making the right that would've took him home he made a left, and headed for the Carrington club. He tried to rationalize it to himself, it was already late, nearly 2:00 a.m.; he wouldn't stay long, just hang-out for a little while. No harm done, Stephanie would never know.

It was impossible to find a parking spot; the regular club patrons, along with the concert crowd, had transformed the lot into one big block party. Eventually, he managed to double-park in the very back. After standing around he decided to walk to the front of club. He casually walked past the long line of cars exiting the parking lot laughing and talking to different girls. He was nearly past the third row of parked cars when he heard a gunshot quickly followed by several more in rapid succession. Chaos ensued as cars sped in all directions and people ran for cover. He ducked and ran with the crowd. It seemed the shooting was coming from somewhere behind him, but he never stopped running long enough to see who was shooting or what they were shooting at. And, he never thought about the shooting again until two months later when two detectives showed up to arrest him. Before then, he wasn't even aware that someone had been killed. But from what the detectives told him, between the months of June and August, he went from being an innocent bystander to the prime suspect.

Now fourteen months later on August 4, 1998, the Honorable Judge Bob Burdette, prosecutor Steve Baldassano, defense attorney Don Irvin, defendant Kenneth West, and 12 jurors were assembled in the 176th District Courtroom to find out why.

Following an opening by the prosecutor, defense attorney Don Irvin said his piece. In his early fifties, he could be described with three words: cool, calm, and collected. He carried himself with a "no reason" to worry demeanor and it appeared that nothing short of a sinking Titanic could unsettle him.

As he began speaking, the defendant looked around the courtroom. His mother, sister, nephew and two childhood friends had turned out to support him; they were seated directly behind the defense table. Across the aisle behind the prosecution was another family composed of two ladies and a young man. They were the only other African Americans in the room which meant they had to be relatives or friends of the deceased. He turned his head back to the front and listened to his attorney.

"Ladies and gentlemen, I expect the evidence will show, as Mr. Baldassano said, that the parking lot out there that night - it's called Carrington's and there was a rap concert at the club, and that when that rap concert ended, people came out of the club. There were 1000 people or so in the parking lot, people were trying to get out, people were standing, milling around. It was a situation where people who were trying to leave the parking lot were there for an hour trying to get out. The parking lot was crowed, it was chaotic, it was nighttime. There will be witnesses who will come and say that Mr. West was in the parking lot that night, and they're right. He was there. That was true. That is true. He was there that night. What's not true is that he pulled a gun and shot into that automobile that had Sammie Johnson in it, and that he killed Sammie Johnson. That is not true. People who come to say that he did shoot that night, that they saw him shoot into that car, are not telling the truth. I'm expecting that the evidence will show that their testimony is incredible; that they could not have seen what they saw; and that is not true that Kenneth West shot Sammie Johnson on June 6th in the parking lot at Carrington's.

That the scene itself was so chaotic, and the circumstances under which the witnesses had an opportunity to view the defendant were so difficult in terms of making an identification, that you will not believe Kenneth West pulled the trigger and shot Sammie Johnson that night. Thank you."

Don Irvin tried to use his argument to summarize several key features of the case; yes, West was in the parking lot, but no, he wasn't a shooter.

The major weakness of his argument was that it made the two witnesses who would testify that they saw the defendant with a gun into liars. While that was certainly a possibility, it ignored what psychologist had showed time and again. Namely, that many other factors besides conscious deception often led to mistaken identifications. Including how long a person had to view an event, stress, information obtained after the event, unconscious transference, biased lineups and suggestiveness by police. Each of these factors can contribute to a mistaken identification and often led to situations where one, ten, even a hundred eye witnesses have been wrong; not consciously lying, just genuinely mistaken.

Such a scientific understanding of various factors that can lead to cases of mistaken identification would've allowed the jurors another option, outside of believing the witnesses were outright lying.

Nevertheless, the defendant could think of several reasons why someone might want to lie on him. The thing in his mind was that he was from the Southeast side of Houston, from an area the young guys called, "South Park." The deceased, as well as the men in his car, and the men scheduled to testify, were all from the, "North side" of Houston. In 1995-97, there was hostility in the black community between these two sides of town, although it was mostly confined to the young male population. Nevertheless, the tension was real and had often boiled over into fight, assaults and gunfire.

Though the origin of these hostilities were unknown, they weren't confined to the streets and often showed up on virulent underground rap tapes where guys from one side of town could be heard dissing and taunting guys from the other.

The defendant had shared this information with his attorney. He believed this South side/North side conflict could be playing a part in his trial as far as the witnesses were concerned.

The state's first four witnesses were HPD officers: T.M Stevens, Joseph Burell, Mark Conner, and Robert Baldwin. They could be considered procedure witnesses as their testimony didn't add any weight to the defendant's guilt or innocence. They basically took the jury through the process and procedures employed whenever a homicide takes place beginning with the initial 911 call.

T.M. Stevens, HPD Patrol Officer

Officer Stevens was first on the scene the night of the shooting. She was with her partner, Officer McDaniels, on patrol when they received the call about a shooting in the Carrington's parking lot.

When the call came, they were two blocks away at the corner of South Main and Buffalo Speedway. It took them approximately two minutes to reach the scene of the shooting and begin securing the area.

The main concession the state obtained from officer Steven's testimony was that no weapons or shell casing were found in the victim's car, thereby planting the "no weapon, innocent victim" seed in the jury's mind early on. But this small victory came at a price as Officer Stevens testified to a few additional facts the prosecutor wasn't quite ready to tackle - the lighting and the crowd.

The state's theory was that the parking lot was extremely well lit and that the average person wouldn't have a problem seeing anyone. Also, the crowd wasn't that excessive; Officer Steven's testimony contradicted this theory.

Q: Was this area better lit than say the average street at night?

A: No, it was not.

Don Irvin appeared surprised by Officer Steven's straight forward answer. Most police officers viewed their jobs and the DA's job as entwined and tended to be evasive when answering questions that could harm the state's case often leading to situations where officers have photographic memories when being questioned by prosecutors, but suddenly become confused, unsure, and forgetful when cross-examined by defense attorneys.

Seeing Officer Stevens hadn't read the script, Don Irvin used her testimony to make another critical point.

Q: Approximately how many people do you think were stranded in that parking lot?

A: I don't think I could give an accurate—

Q: Ball park? More than 500?

A: At least 800 cars.

Q: There was 800 cars? So, there had to be at least 800 people? And, there were a lot of people who were not in cars?

A: Yes, there were.

Q: And, in many of the cars there were lots of people? I mean, there was more than one person in many of the cars?

A: Yes.

By the time Officer Stevens left the witness stand, Don Irvin was extremely pleased. In his opening statement, he told the jury the parking lot was chaotic and Officer Steven's testimony supported that assertion. Criminal Defense Lawyering 101 said that whatever a lawyer promised a jury, he had better be able to Deliver; if not, he would lose credibility with the jury. People hated being lied to and jurors were people which meant they often had the same expectations of lawyers as other people they dealt with; if you said it, you had to Deliver.

Joseph Burell, HPD Officer

In rapid succession following Officer Stevens, was fourteen year police veteran Officer Burell, a Crime Scene officer. He told the jury he arrived on the scene around 3:00 AM and went through the process of securing the evidence which included labeling and photographing individual shell casings, casings he believed originated from several different guns. At that point, a TV was wheeled into the courtroom and a video of the scene that included the deceased was shown to the jury.

But it was something else that Officer Burell said that piqued the defendant's interest and made him nudge his attorney. Officer Burell had testified that when he arrived on the scene, he noted 50 or 60 witnesses talking to homicide Detectives Vacaras and Abbondondolo. Where were these 50 or 60 witnesses? The defendant was on trial because two friends of the victim had identified him as a shooter, but it was obvious to him that none of these 50 or 60 witnesses had identified him as a shooter or else they would've been present to testify. However, if these witnesses saw the shooting, had anyone made an effort to see if they could be used to exclude him? It became apparent that this hadn't been done; the detectives were only interested in witnesses who would put a gun in his hand.

From the prosecutor's standpoint, Officer Burrell was the perfect prosecution witnesses. He said the lighting in the parking lot was so good he didn't have to use a flash when he photographed the spent shell casings, and although the pictures presented to the jury were a little grainy, that was only because he used what he called, "Natural Light."

The last assertion led to a spat with the defense attorney.

Q: That was going to be my question; you do not use a flash, but you used a high-speed film, did you not?

A: 400 film yes.

Q: Okay. And, 400 film gathers more light then 100 film; I'm talking about ASA?

A: Correct.

Don Irvin continued to press this point for several minutes. Finally, he moved on to the video camera Officer Burell used to make the tape the jury had just seen. Officer Burell admitted the camera had a light attached to it that threw about eight feet of light. Don Irvin considered this an "Ah ha," moment and looked over at the jury. Did they get that? If the jury got it, his client didn't. He thought his lawyer was kicking a dead horse.

Assuming the jurors had the average amount of intellect, they pretty much knew how a strip center parking lot looked at 2:00 in the morning, with slight variations, if you had seen one, you pretty much had seen them all.

But, for Don Irvin, the point was significant. He wanted the jury to know: Hey these pictures look pretty good and so does the video, but this not really how the parking lot looked at that time of night; it was much, much darker.

Right when it seemed he was about to launch into another round of questions about the intricacies of film speed and light exposure, he abruptly changed the subject.

Q: Now I was a little bit confused by your testimony about the cartridge cases. How many different types of cases were there? How many different calibers?

A: There were three different types of casings.

Q: Okay. There was 9-millmeter?

A: There was 9-millmeter?

Q: How many 9-millimeters were there?

A: I have to count them. I have 19 9-millimeter cases.

Q: And .40 caliber, how many of those?

A: Make that 20-9 millimeter and seven .40 caliber.

Q: Twenty 9-millimeter and seven .40 calibers?

A: That's correct.

Q: And, then the other caliber was what?

A: It was a rifle slug. It had WCC 92 on the back of it. I don't know the size of it.

Q: It was a rifle?

A: Correct, a rifle casing.

Baldassano looked like he had been struck by lightning. Up until that point, Officer Burell had been a perfect witness. He quickly realized his mistake and tried to do damage control.

Q: You said something about a rifle?

A: No, I'm sorry. I was going by the WCC. That's usually a rifle stamping on the back of it. Each piece of ammunition has got a stamping on the back of the cartridge case, on the face.

West was on the edge of his seat. What was the prosecution hiding? He looked at Officer Burell. Now the previously poised 14 year HPD veteran was scrambling to undo his mistake. The evidence couldn't be allowed to speak for itself, because it might not say the right thing. At this point Don Irvin did something his client really admired; he let the officer talk.

Q: Uh -huh

A: Okay, most of your .40 caliber, your .45 caliber, your 9- millimeter, your .380, your .25, all that kind of stuff, have a brand name, whatever it may be, and then, like 9-millimeter it may be, and then, like 9-millimeter Luger, .45 automatic, .380 auto. In this case, this casing has WCC 92. That's all it has on the back of it. Normally, that's for a rifle casing so when I looked at my report, that's what I saw. It looks like a rifle casing, but it's actually a cartridge casing, probably a 9-millimeter that was manufactured outside the United States.

Q: But, you don't know?

A I don't know for certain.[3]

Mark Conner, HPD Officer

Next up was another HPD Veteran, Mark Conner. He was in charge of the physical inspection of the older model, light blue Delta 88 in which the deceased was riding. He testified that during his inspection of the vehicle at the HPD impound garage, he didn't find any weapons in the car and that most of the gunshot impact was to the back of the car on the driver's side. In all, he collected twenty to twenty-five bullet fragments. That was the extent of Officer Conner's testimony. Baldassano was basically telling the jury, "Hey, these guys didn't have a gun, at least not one that was found." But considering that three of the four men in the car had criminal histories involving firearms, unless a leopard could change its' stripes, it was unlikely that they weren't armed.

Robert Baldwin, HPD Officer

Robert Baldwin was the HPD firearm expert and the last of the procedural witnesses. A good portion of Mr. Baldwin's testimony was spent dazzling the jury with his long list of credentials. "My formal education consists of a Bachelor of Science degree as well as a Jurist Doctorate degree. I've been in the field of criminalistics for approaching 20 years

[3]In officer Burrell's original reported he noted the recovery of a white and blue number 21 jersey. A subsequent witnesses would testify that the shooters he saw had jersey's with numbers on them/nevertheless the connection between this testimony and the jersey recovered at the crime scene was never explored.

now and better than 10 of that has been in firearms-related work. I've received specialized training at the FBI, the ATF, Smith & Wesson Arms, Colt Arms, Remington Arms, Sig Arms, Glock Arms. I've also done course work in forensic microscopy at Krohn institute."

Absent from the list was why the HPD Ballistic lab was in the news a few years later for shoddy ballistic work.

When the erudite Mr. Baldwin finished enumerating his credentials, he explained to the jury how semi-automatic guns work, how fired shell cases ejected and how far they were likely to travel (five to seven feet) from the gun. He went on to say that from his examination of the spent shell casings, he determined three different guns were used: two 9-millimeters and a .40 Cal. And although no weapons were ever recovered by the police, he went ahead and speculated on the types of weapons likely used. The 9-millimeters were likely a Beretta and Taurus, while the 40. Cal was most likely a Glock. Of course this was only his expert opinion based on his extensive experience.

Then to make sure the jury knew how a semi-automatic weapon looked, Mr. Baldwin produced his own 9-millimeter Taurus that he had borrowed from the property room. Soon as the gun came out, Don Irvin was on his feet. "For the purpose of the record, ladies and gentlemen, so that you well know, State's exhibit 91 that being the weapon Mr. Baldwin is currently holding for demonstrative purposes only, has been admitted for your consideration."

With the conclusion of the first four witnesses, Baldassano had succeeded in establishing several facets of the State's case: On June 6, 1997 a car with four men in a club parking lot was shot multiple times and a man was killed. According to the Crime Scene investigator, the light in the parking lot wasn't as good as daylight, but it was still pretty good. A subsequent search of the victim's vehicle failed to produce any weapons, and three separate guns were fired, most likely a Berretta, a Taurus, and a Glock.

Across the aisle Don Irvin was tallying his own victories: On the night Sammie Johnson was killed, Carrington's parking lot was extremely crowded; more crowded than usual with one thousand to fifteen hundred people and eight hundred cars. The parking lot lighting couldn't have been that great if the Crime Scene investigator had to use a special type of light-sensitive film for photos and a light bulb to make a video. A bullet shell that could've come from a rifle was found. And ballistic evidence pointed to three guns, meaning there were likely three shooters, not two as the prosecutor theorized to the jury.

The jury trial of The State of Texas vs. West was now in its second day and though the defendant had taken judicious notes, he was confused by the process. This was his first time facing felony charges and he was eager to find out what the testimony he had just heard had to do with him?

Jerome Sampson

Twenty year old Jerome Sampson was the state's next witness. At this point, the state began moving into what would be the meat and potatoes of its case against the defendant.

Dressed in dark jeans and a polo-style shirt, Mr. Sampson walked to the witness stand. It was immediately apparent, he didn't have warm feelings for the defendant though neither knew the other personally, they got into a kind of macho staring match that prompted Don Irvin to chide his client, "Stop that."

Baldassano used his first question to reveal to the jury that Mr. Sampson had a minor criminal record consisting of auto-theft and marijuana possession.

After diffusing this potential time bomb, he moved on to the night of June 6, 1997. Mr. Sampson said he went to the Carrington's Club around 11:30 or 12:00 a.m. with his three friends, Sammie Ray Johnson, Robert Levi, and Carl Anderson.[4] They didn't go in the club, instead opting to stay out in the parking lot. According to Mr. Sampson, they all lived in the same apartment complex and were just hanging out. He was driving, Carl Anderson was in the passenger seat, Sammie Ray Johnson was behind him and Robert Levi was sitting next to Sammie. He said they didn't have any guns nor had they been smoking or drinking anything. Neither did they have any type of confrontation with anyone while out in the parking lot.

Once this was established, Baldassano led Mr. Sampson to the shooting.

Q: Okay, were you parked in a parking space or were you waiting to get out?

A: I was waiting to get out.

Q: Okay, and were there a lot of cars around?

A: Yeah.

Q: Were there a lot of people around?

---

[4]Jerome Sampson, Robert Levi, and Carl Anderson's future actions seemed to fly in the face of their "Innocent Victim" claim. As each continued to rack up and long list of arrest and criminal convictions in the months and years following the defendant's trial.

A: Uh-huh.

Q: Were there lights over there?

A: Yeah, there was lights

Q: Before the shooting started or after the shooting started, or during the shooting, did you ever see the defendant?

A: Yeah.

Q: Okay, when you saw the defendant, can you explain where you saw him and what, if anything, you saw him doing?

A: When I was leaving up there by Carrington's, I seen him walk on the side of my car; my driver's side.

Q: Were you parked at the time waiting to get out?

A: Yeah.

Q: You already told us about where your car was parked when the shooting started. Was it there or somewhere else that you saw the defendant?

A: When I was leaving the exit, when I was going toward the Stop and Go, that's when I seen him.

Q: Roughly how long before the shooting did you see him?

A: Not that long. Three or four minutes, five minutes at the most.

Q: When you saw him, what did you see him do, if anything?

A: Just walk by my car.

Q: Did you see who did the shooting?

A: No, sir.

On his legal pad, the defendant scribbled, "What made him notice me out of the hundreds of other people walking past his car?" and showed it to his attorney.

West had told his lawyer that he walked past the cars exiting the parking lot, but didn't pay attention to them unless they were occupied by females. Therefore, it was possible he had walked past Mr. Sampson and his party without realizing it.

Once the shooting began, Mr. Sampson testified he mashed the accelerator in an attempt to get away and ended up crashing into another car before coming to a stop beside the Stop N Go where he sought help. In the process of seeking help, his friend Jessie Brown[5] came across the street and they had an interesting conversation. Referring to Mr. Brown he said, "My homeboy, Jessie, he came back, he came in and asked me, you know, what happened, what we had did. And I was like, I don't know. I was trying to ask him did he know why he was shooting at us."

During the pre-trial investigation, it was alleged that Mr. Sampson and his friends were known car-jackers who had likely been in the Carrington's parking lot looking to hit a lick, street slang for committing a robbery. The defense believed that if this was the case, it was quite possible that

[5]This is the same Jessie Brown who would later identity the defendant as one of the shooters.

someone they had robbed, or attempted to rob, had spotted them and decided to seek revenge.

In his cross-examination, Don Irvin tried to put this information before the jury.

Q: You got there at 11:30 or 12:00, is that correct?

A: Correct.

Q: So, you were … what were you doing in the parking lot almost an hour or something?

A: Just riding around.

Q: Well how many people were out there?

A: I don't know; a thousand, two - I don't know; something like that.

Q: Did you see any cars out there that night that attracted your attention?

A: No.

Q: What about a Red Lincoln?

A: Yeah, I saw that car out there.

Q: And, what was it about that car that attracted your attention?

A: Because the dude that drives that car, he's a rapper.

Q: Yeah?

A: So, I mean I had seen the car before.

Q: And, what was it that happened with relationship to you and that car?

A: There wasn't really no relationship with it. All I know is it was a red Lexus out there and a red Lincoln out there. And after I got shot, that car was gone. When I got out of my car to see what was going on, that car had left. But the Lexus was still there and I'm pretty sure the two cars were together.

Before Mr. Sampson left the stand, Don Irvin was able to score a victory for the defense on the issue of identity. Throughout the trial the witnesses were saying they saw the defendant Kenneth West, yet they all seemed to have seen a different Kenneth West beginning with Mr. Sampson.

On June 12th, the day of Mr. Johnson's funeral, Mr. Sampson went to the police station at the behest of detective Abbondondolo. After being interviewed, he was shown a photo spread in which he picked the defendant as someone he had seen in the parking lot. Following this identification, he wrote a statement in which he said the defendant was wearing the same shirt in the photo spread as he was the night he saw him, a red Nautica t-shirt.[6]

But on the witnesses stand he tried to distance himself from this point, and became so contentious that Don Irvin had to ask him to reread his original statement.

---

[6]Mr. Sampson's original statement has been reprinted in Appendix 1

The juror watched and Don Irvin waited while he read his statement. When he finished, Don Irvin asked again about the defendant's attire on the night of the shooting.

Q: Well, did you say, I think he was wearing the same shirt that night that he was in the picture?

A: Yeah.

Lawrence Fields

In keeping with the theme of using each successive witness to reveal more information than the previous one, Baldassano called twenty-year old Lawrence Fields to the stand. Mr. Fields testimony was different from the other witnesses in that he didn't attend the Boxopooloza concert, nor did he go to the Carrington Club. Instead, he was a passerby stuck in traffic on Westgate with his Kroger's co-worker, Tracy Dion Gravett.[7]

The duo was on their way to Jack-In-The-Box when suddenly to their left, shots rang out. Tracy noticed it first and screamed, "They shooting," then she attempted to duck. Fearing for his safety, Mr. Fields said his first thought was to let his seat back, but the seat was broken. So in an effort to protect himself and Ms. Gravett[7], he leaned forward on top of her.

In that instant, from a hundred feet away, he looked into the parking lot and saw the defendant dressed in dark pants and a light colored shirt; or at least he though he did. In the initial statement he gave officer Varchris

[7]Ms.Gravett didn't testify, however, she was interviewed by detectives; her original statement has been reprinted in Appendix 1

after being shown the photo spread, he wasn't certain, telling detectives the defendant, "looked like," the guy he saw. He also said he was having trouble determining the suspect's size. This prompted detective Varchris to ask him if he would be more comfortable seeing the suspect in a live line-up, and he said he would. A line-up was never conducted and the detectives classified Mr. Fields' identification as "tentative" in their report. Nevertheless, in the months that ensued, Mr. Fields' uncertainty, miraculous transformed into certainty; now he was positive.

Unfortunately, this certainty didn't extend to other areas of his initial recollection, particularly not when it came to what the shooters were wearing or the vehicle they got into. In his original sworn statement it was a Suburban, but now on the witness stand, he wasn't sure.

Q: Now when you talked to Officer Abby, you told him a couple of things about identifying features of the person you saw, didn't you?

A: Yeah

Q: You told him that they were wearing dark pants and caps.

A: What I told him was one of them was like a tall, dark-skinned heavy set dude and the other one was a little bit thinner than him, shorter and brighter.

Q: Okay.

A: And that they had on some dark pants and light colored shirts.

Q: Okay, did you tell him that both of them had on dark pants and caps?

A: I don't remember caps.

Q: You don't remember caps. Do you remember telling him that two guys got into a suburban? That the two guys you saw got into a Suburban?

Apparently he didn't and for the second time, Don Irvin had to confront a prosecution witness with his initial statement[8] that had been given days after the shooting. Reluctantly, he agreed to this recollection. Exactly why Mr. Fields suddenly wanted to change his testimony at the points that conflicted with the state's theory was a mystery to the defendant.

Jerome Sampson had basically done the same thing but his reasons were clear. His friend had been killed and he thought, or at the very least had been told, the defendant did it; undoubtedly he wanted to see him punished.

But what was Mr. Fields' angle? It was revealed during testimony that he had once gone to school with and was acquainted with the deceased. Yet it was more likely the answer was found in the response he gave Mr. Irvin when questioned about his original statement.

Q: Okay. Can you tell me whether or not you told Officer Vacaras that the persons out there who were shooting, that both had on dark pants and caps?

A: I don't remember caps because they asked me. They (Homicide detectives) said anything on like their heads or stuff like that? I probably told him yeah, but I don't know.

[8]Mr. Fields' original statement has been reprinted in Appendix 1

Mr. Fields appeared to possess a strong desire to be a good witness and to be as helpful to the detectives as possible to the point of agreeing to something the detective said, even if it wasn't true. "I probably told him yeah, but I don't know."

While Mr. Fields' testimony placed the defendant at the scene, he admitted that he only saw him for a few seconds, and in that few seconds, he didn't see him with a gun.

A We heard gunshots and that's what she said, so I kind of looked over for a couple of seconds because at first, I thought somebody was shooting a gun in the air or something.

Q: All right. You looked over for a couple of seconds?

A: Yeah.

Q: And how many shots were fired while you were looking over there?

A: I don't know.

Q: Couple?

A: About five or six; somewhere like that.

Q: Okay. And you did not see this man with a gun out there that night, did you?

A: I couldn't really see him with a gun because he was standing behind the car.

Q: Well, that's my question, did you see him with a gun.

A: No.

Had Kenneth West been the only person in the parking lot with the victims, Mr. Fields' testimony might have been feasible. But with bumper-to-bumper traffic in both directions on Westgate and a parking lot with eight hundred cars, and one thousand to fifteen hundred people, exactly how he managed to look over from a hundred feet and spot the defendant, or anyone else, in a few second glance without his glasses was a mystery.

Nevertheless, Mr. Fields' testimony highlighted two facts that went to the heart of the case. The first had to do with the type of investigation that was conducted by detective Abbondondlo and Vachris.

When asked about his identification of the defendant, Mr. Fields made a curious statement.

Q: And did he give you any instructions before you looked at the group of pictures?

A: Just to pick out who I thought resembled whoever I saw around there that night.

Thought? Resembled? In their zeal to build a case, homicide detectives were no longer interested in positive identifications, but resemblances? It's doubtful many Americans would like to stand trial for murder based on what a witness thought or who they resembled. As it applied to Mr. Fields, such an outrageously low-standard wasn't particularly harmful to the defendant. However if, "thought" and "resembled" were the same standard the detectives used with the following witnesses, Larry Risher and Jessie Brown, witnesses who put a gun in the defendant's hand, then such an unreliable standard was undoubtedly catastrophic for the defendant.

The second factor revealed from Mr. Fields' testimony was overlooked in the hustle and bustle of cross-examination. Normal police procedure was to use whatever evidence available to lead to a suspect. But in the West case, the process was reversed. Suspects were selected then evidence was amassed in an attempt to prove their guilt.

Sammie Ray Johnson was killed on June 6, 1997; the defendant wasn't identified as a shooter by Jessie Brown and Larry Risher until months later; a month and a half for Brown, and three for Risher. Therefore, from June 6th till the end of August, the police didn't have any evidence connecting the defendant to the shooting. But on June 12th, six days after the shooting a month before anyone had identified the defendant, homicide detectives were showing a photo spread that contained the defendant and his co-defendant's picture to Jerome Sampson and Lawrence Fields; at the time, they had no evidence connecting the defendant to Mr. Johnson's death. No witnesses, surveillance footage, fingerprints, guns, nothing. None of that mattered; he was already their prime suspect. If they didn't have proof, then they would get it.

<u>Larry Risher</u>

And that's exactly what they did. Throughout the trial, the most damaging testimony against the defendant came from 20 year old Larry Risher and his 24 year old friend Jessie Brown. At first glance, their testimony made it an open and shut case; both positively identified the defendant as one of the men they saw shooting. But under closer scrutiny, their testimonies begin to unravel.

Mr. Risher was first on the stand. He attended the Boxopooloza concert with his friends Jessie Brown and Yattie Gordon. After hanging out at the concert for two hours, they left in Mr. Risher's Impala Super Sport and went to hangout some more in Carrington's parking lot. The reason for this was that Mr. Risher was only twenty years old, too young to drink or get into Carrington's.

They arrived in the parking lot around 12:30 or 1:00 am and parked in front of the tire shop. For a potential witness, this was the ideal parking spot as it turned out to be directly in front of were three or four gunmen attacked Jerome Sampson's car.

According to Mr. Risher, one of these gunmen was the defendant Kenneth West, a man he had previously seen 10 to 15 times in other clubs.

When asked about the defendant's actions, Mr. Risher testified.

Q: And what was he doing?

A: He was coming up on the car and I didn't stick around to see the outcome after the shooting started.

Q: Did you see the defendant shoot?

A: Yes, sir.

Q: What did you see him do?

A: Point at the back of the car and shoot.

Q: And how many shots did you watch as the defendant was shooting?

A: Maybe one or two; around one or two.

Q: And then what happened?

A: I ran to the back of the building, ran around the side of the tire station.

West was floored. Here he was face-to-face with a man who was testifying to something he knew was impossible, that he had shot and killed Sammie Johnson. The feeling and emotional suffering experienced by an innocent person who has to sit passively while being accused of a crime they didn't commit is incomprehensible. In that moment, it appeared all of the defendant's strength and resolve left him and his shoulders visibly slumped. Unnerved, he looked at his mother.

At the time, he knew nothing about unconscious transference, or how innocent bystanders were frequently wrongfully identified by witnesses. In a trance, he studied the details of Mr. Risher's round, brown face while searching the crevices of his mind to try to remember if he had ever seen him before. If he had, he couldn't remember, which unnerved him even more.

Thus far, this was the most important testimony he had heard and he hung onto every word Mr. Risher said; his life depended on it.

On direct, Mr. Risher's testimony appeared iron-clad, but on cross-examination, it began to fall apart. That was the first time the defendant allowed himself to breath. While he knew he didn't shoot Mr. Johnson, what was important was for the jury to know it.

Don Irvin rose for cross-examination.

Q: Did you give him that statement on September 23, 1997?

A: Yes, sir.

Q: So, that's really … that's really more than three months after the shooting, isn't it?

A: Yes sir.

Q: Now, you say you saw the defendant out there. How was he dressed?

A: I really couldn't tell you sir.

Q: You don't know what kind of clothes he had on or anything?

A: Looked like a Polo or something. A Polo shirt, I really couldn't tell you.

Q: Well, think about it. It was three months until you identified him in the photo spread?

A: I identified him because I had seen him before.

Most psychologists versed in the field of "eyewitness testimony" would've kicked Don Irvin for not getting the witness to elaborate on this statement, "I identified him because I had seen him before." Baring outright lying, Risher's testimony was consistent with many of the factors experts have proven lead to mistaken identifications.

Q: Well, if you don't remember the type of clothing he had on, do you remember any colors?

A: No, sir.

Q: Do you remember whether or not he had a hat on?

A: Nope. No, sir.

Q: So, you don't know anything?

Q: About how he was dressed?

A: No, sir.

Q: Do you remember anything any of the shooters were wearing?

A: No, sir.

Q: How many shooters did you say there were?

A: Three or four.

Q: There were three or four?

A: Yes, sir.

Q: Okay. Now, do I understand your testimony on direct correctly that you didn't talk to anybody out there that night about what happened?

A: No, sir.I did not talk to no one.

Q: To no one? Okay. You didn't talk to the police officers? Didn't talk to anybody?

A: Yes, sir.

Q: And, when you decided to leave, who did you leave with?

A: Jessie Brown and the other person who rode with me.

Q: Who was that?

A: A dude named Yattie.

Q: How do you spell that?

A: Y-a-t-i.

Q: You know what his last name is?

A: No, sir.

Q: How do you know him?

A: From the neighborhood.

Q: Does he live near you?

A: No, I don't know where he stay?

Q: Okay, so the three of you got in the car and left? Jessie Brown, Yattie and you?

A: Yes, sir.

Q: And Jessie Brown had seen the shooting?

A: Yes, sir.

Q: Correct? And you had seen the shooting?

A: Yes, sir.

Q: Is that right? And you're telling me and this jury that you and Jessie Brown didn't talk about the shooting?

A: Not until we left. We was at home.

Q: And, you and Jessie Brown talked about the shooting?

A: Yes, we talked about which way we ran. We didn't talk about nothing else, like--the only thing we asked each other is "who did we see?" "Did we see who shot?"

Q: You didn't talk about that man, that guy, Kenneth West, that you see everywhere? You didn't talk about did you see him out there?

A: I didn't know his name. I am pretty sure Jessie didn't know his name.

Q: You didn't tell Jessie you knew who the shooter was?

A: No.

Q: In the three months/you didn't tell anybody you knew who the shooter was?

A: No, sir.

Q: You kept that to yourself?

A: Yes.

Q: You knew Sammie Johnson?

A: Yes, sir.

Q: Sammie Johnson was a friend of yours?

A: Yes, sir.

Q: You didn't want, during those three months, to let the police know who shot him?

A: They told me they had arrested him. I thought they already had him in custody, so it wasn't no reason.

Q: You weren't in the least bit curious about whether or not they had the right man in custody?

A: No, sir.

Q: You weren't?

A: No, sir.

Q: It never occurred to you they might have the wrong man?

A: No, sir.

Q: You said that Sammie Johnson was you friend, so you had to to get involved?

A: Yes, sir.

Q: Somebody had to call you, didn't they?

A: Yes, sir.

Q: You didn't get involved until three months later?

A: Yes, sir.

The jury looked at the defendant; it appeared they were all thinking the same thing. Something wasn't right. This man allegedly saw his friend killed by someone he knew but didn't talk to the police until three months later when they contacted him. He said he saw three or four shooters, but could only identify two, the same two homicide detectives were building another case on and conveniently adding their pictures to every photo spread they could.

Even more incredible was Mr. Risher testified that he drove home with two other friends who had all witnessed another friend Sammie Johnson get killed, and they didn't discuss what happened, or who they saw.[9]

His testimony had stopped making sense. What sane, rational person would watch their friend get killed by someone they knew; not contact the police, or discuss it with other friends who witnessed it, and not be able to describe anything about the shooters, except what the police showed him, their faces?

---

[9]As discussed in Chapter 8, the ability of one witness to influence another such as when one says in the hearing of the other, "He had the bluest eyes I've ever seen," is a well documented phenomenon called, "post event information." Since both Mr. Risher and Mr. Brown were adamant that they didn't discuss what they had seen, which is contrary to logic, it appears they received some pre-trial coaching from the DA on this important issue.

Jessie Brown

Baldassano didn't waste any time with 24 year old Jessie Brown .Like everybody involved in the West trial he didn't drink, or do drugs, which might've been true in his case since he was the only person to testify who had a job.

After walking him through the basics of who he was with, and what time they arrived the prosecutor jumped right in.

Q: Did you see Sammie? Do you know Sammie Ray Johnson, Jr?

A: Yes.

Q: How do you know him?

A: Went to school with him.

Q: How long have you known him?

A: I'd say about eight or nine years.

Q: When they pulled up did they get out of the car?

A: No.

Q: Did they stop?

A: Yes.

Q: Did you talk to anybody in the car?

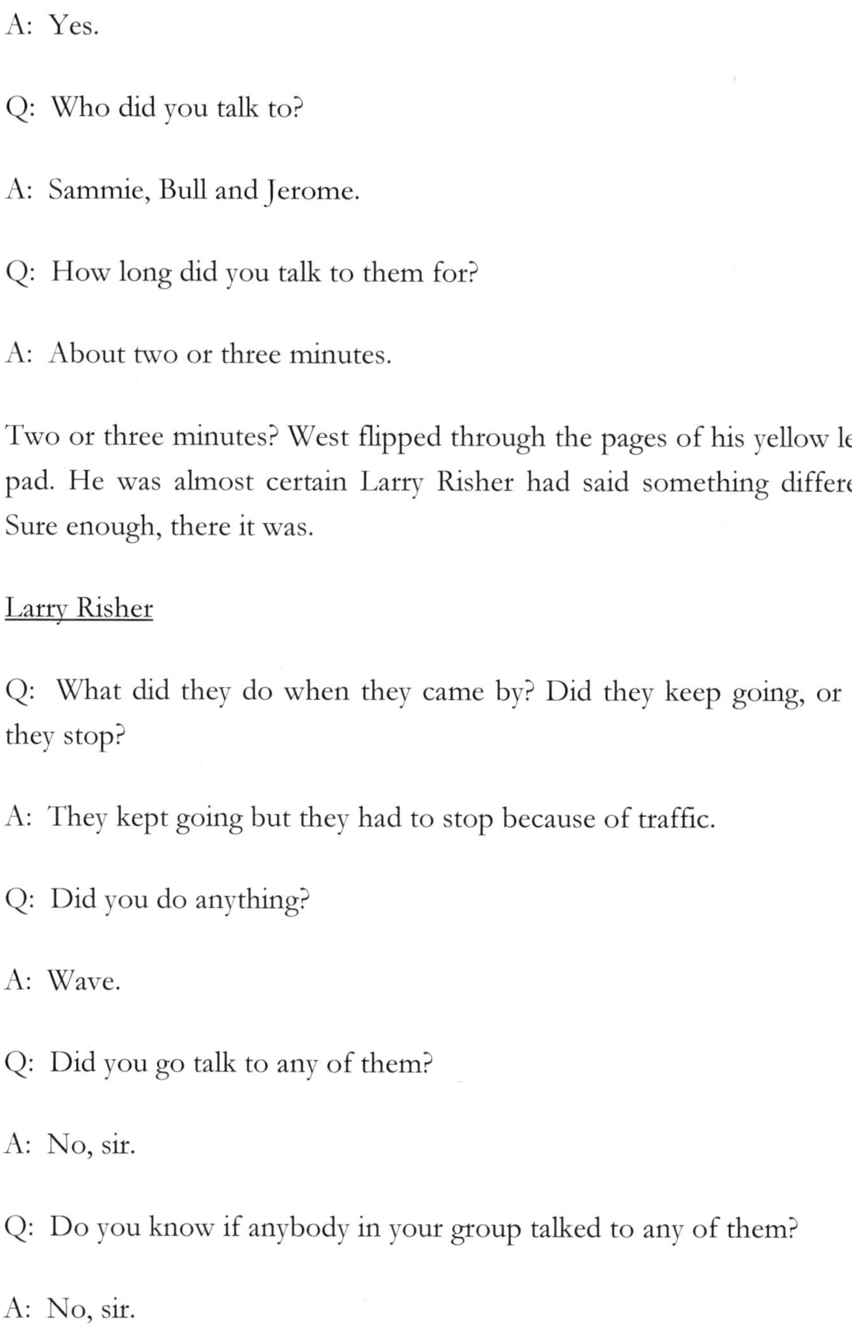

A: Yes.

Q: Who did you talk to?

A: Sammie, Bull and Jerome.

Q: How long did you talk to them for?

A: About two or three minutes.

Two or three minutes? West flipped through the pages of his yellow legal pad. He was almost certain Larry Risher had said something different. Sure enough, there it was.

<u>Larry Risher</u>

Q: What did they do when they came by? Did they keep going, or did they stop?

A: They kept going but they had to stop because of traffic.

Q: Did you do anything?

A: Wave.

Q: Did you go talk to any of them?

A: No, sir.

Q: Do you know if anybody in your group talked to any of them?

A: No, sir.

As he continued looking at his tablet and notes he saw more inconsistencies.

Q: How many shooters?

<u>Larry Risher</u>

A: Three or four.

<u>Jessie Brown</u>

Q: Now, I believe you said there were two shooters, is that correct?

A: Yes.

What were the shooters wearing?

<u>Larry Risher</u>

Q: Now, you say you saw the defendant out there. How was he dressed?

A: Looked like a Polo or something. Polo shirt--I really couldn't tell you.

<u>Lawrence Fields</u>

Q: You told him that they were wearing dark pants and caps?

A: And, they had on some dark pants and light colored shirts.

<u>Jessie Brown</u>

Q: What were these two shooters that you saw wearing out there that night?

A: Football jerseys.

Q: They were wearing football jerseys?

A: Yes.

Q: Both of them were?

A: A burgundy and a blue one.

Q: Okay, and they had numbers on them?

A: Yeah.

West nudged his attorney and showed him what he was looking at. Either these people witnessed two different shooting, or one didn't witness the shooting at all and was simply acting on second hand information. Now he understood why Baldassano went through the elaborate scenario during Voir Dire about the bailiff. There was a good chance that his witnesses were identifying the wrong person.

The defendant focused on the jury. Studied the men and women in charge of his fate and tried to read their minds. He wanted to know if they saw the inconsistencies, because if they didn't, they didn't matter.

In a jury trial the truth was whatever looked like the truth. All the the prosecutor had to do was make a defendant look guilt. If he succeed in doing that the jury would do the rest; innocent or not.

And in that one aspect Baldassano appeared to be succeeding.

Q: While you were talking to the guys in the car, did anything happen?

A: Yes.

Q: What happened?

A: Two guys ran up from the back and started shooting.

Q: Do you see one of those guys in the courtroom?

A: Yes.

Q: How close were you to Sammie's car or Jerome's car when the shooting started?

A: About ten feet?[10]

Q: Were you talking to them when the shooting started?

A: Yes, spoke to him.

Q: Were you actively engaged in a conversation form 10 feet away, or you just —

A: Spoke to him and then I heard boom. When I heard that, I ran in front of the car, and the man in the dark suit, him and his partner were standing side by side shooting.

Q: Sir, I'm going to show you what's been labeled as State Exhibit No.91 for demonstration only. Does this look similar to the type of gun?

A: Yes

[10]Robert Baldwin the HPD firearm expert testified that three guns were fired, leading to the logical conclusion that there were three gunmen. If Jessie Brown was only ten feet away as he testified, then how was it that he only saw two shooters?

Q: After the shooting ended, what's the next thing you do?

A: Ran across the street where the car was.

Q: Which car was that?

A: Sammie's, Jerome's car.

Jessie Brown's testimony disturbed the defendant the most. He said he was positive the defendant was a shooter. As positive as the defendant was that he wasn't.

However, Mr. Brown's testimony was plagued by the same lapses and unexplained actions as Mr. Risher's making it nearly impossible to distinguish the fact from the fiction.

Q: Now, when the gunfire started, were you frightened at all?

A: No.

Q: It didn't scare you when people started shooting?

A: No.

Q: Larry Risher is a pretty good friend of yours, isn't he?

A: Yes.

Q: You haven't discussed this case together during this trial?

A: No.

Q: Now, I believe you testified on direct examination that you knew Sammie Johnson?

A: Yes.

Q: Were you friends?

A: Yes.

Q: And you liked him?

A: Yes, I loved him.

Q: You loved him?

A: Yes.

Q: Okay, and what about the other guys in the car?

A: Jerome?

Q: Jerome, Robert Levi and Carl Anderson. Did you know those guys?

A: Yes

Q: Do you care about him as much as you do Sammie?

A: About the same.

Q: What about Robert Levi.

A: The same.

Q: Okay, is it safe to say you loved all these guys?

A: Yes.

Q: Okay, out there that night, after you held Jerome in your arms, you got up and left, or you got up to leave; did you see any police officers out there?

A: No.

Q: Did you ever see police officers out there that night?

A: Yes.

Q: You left as soon as the police got there?

A: No, not as soon as I saw, but I left.

Q: Well, at any rate, you were there during the period of time that the police were there, isn't that true?

A: When they got there I left.

Q: Okay, but there was a period of time that you were there?

A: Yes.

Q: During that period of time, did you have any desire at all to walk up to any of those police officers and tell them who it was that shot and killed your friend?

A: No.

Q: That you loved?

A: No.

Q: Why not?

A: I was mad, angry; shook up.

Q: Well, can you tell the jury why when you're mad and shook up you don't turn to the police and tell them who just killed…who just murdered your friend.

A: No.

Q: You have no explanation for that?

A: No.

Q: Now, when you left out there that evening, you left with Larry Risher, did you not?

A: Yes.

Q: And, you left in the Impala Super sport?

A: Yes.

Q: And, when you got in the car did you discuss…

A: No

Q: …the murder that just happened.

A: No.

Q: So, at the very least you spent about 30 minutes or a half an hour in the car with Mr. Risher?

A: Yes.

Q: And, during that period of time, you didn't discuss this shooting at all.

A: No

Q: Okay. Now, during the period of time between when you got out of the car that night at home and the police contacting you two months later--

A: Uh-huh.

Q: Did you talk to anybody about having seen the shooter who shot your friend?

A: No

Q: Why didn't you do that?

A: For what?

Q: You wouldn't be interested in seeing the person who shot and killed your friend get prosecuted?

A: Yes.

Q: During that same period of time, between the time that you left the shooting out there, the scene of the shooting out there and you were dropped off at home that night, that same night or morning, did you ever try to contact some of these friends that you love - Jerome Sampson and Robert Levi - and tell them what you knew?

A: Yes.

Q: What did you do?

A: I went to their house and seen them.

Q: Well, I understand. How long was this after the incident itself that you went and talked to your friends?

A: The next day.

Q: Okay. But after having seen them, did you then go and try to contact the police?

A: They contacted me.

Q: Okay. And then it took two months after that before the police contacted you?

A: Yeah, they couldn't find me.

Q: My question is, you wanted to see the persons who murdered your friend, and shot your other friends, and knowing that your testimony, why didn't you go to the police? Why did they have to seek you out?

A: I don't know.

Q: You have no explanation for that?

A: No.

C.P. Abbondondolo, Homicide Detective

If one person had a major role in the case of the State of Texas vs. West, it was homicide detective C.P. Abbondondolo. Due to the difficulty most people encounter when attempting to pronounce his name he was often referred to simply as detective Abby. A folksy man with a serious demeanor he had an easy going way that tended to endear him with people, yet he was every bit of a cop's cop.

Detective Abby arrived in the Carrington's parking lot at 3:00 am with his partner Ken Vacaras. Together, they did a walk-through of the scene that included an examination of the deceased along with his vehicle and a brief interview of witnesses remaining at the scene.

Their next stop was the hospital where the three passengers had been taken. Here he encountered a road block as the victim/witnesses didn't want to talk to him.

The reasons for this weren't entirely clear, but eventually he was able to get the names of Jessie Brown and Larry Risher as potential witnesses.

Nearly two months later he caught up with Jessie Brown at his aunt's house. Mr. Brown was reluctant to speak with him, but after impressing upon him the seriousness of the incident he said Mr. Brown agreed to give him a statement. Following his statement detective Abby showed a photo based line-up that he had with him and Mr. Brown picked the defendant out of the line-up.

Unfortunately the circumstances under which this identification took place weren't videotaped leaving the defendant and his attorney to take the detectives' word concerning the process that led to Mr. Brown's identification. As they had no way of determining how suggestive the process was or if detective Abby did anything to influence it either overtly, or covertly.

After Mr. Brown's identification another month passed before the detective was able to get in touch with Larry Risher who he said again identified the defendant as one of the shooters.

Baldassano asked him about the identifications.

Q: Well, what did you observe when he made those selections was he tentative, negative, or positive?

A: He was positive. I don't believe he was as positive as the other witness was, but he was right on the money as far there was no questions. He spent a little more time looking at the pictures.

Although detective Abby characterized the identifications as positive both were problematic.

The process by which police show witnesses a photo spread containing a potential suspect is essentially a experiment. An experiment where the hypothesis, or theory of the officer conducting the investigation is that the actually perpetrator of the crime is among the pictures being shown.

But, because the design of the experiment is flawed, the results wouldn't be accepted anywhere in the scientific community. The scientific literature is ripe with information of how the experimenter (in this case the police) can influence the results, i.e. who the witness identifies in subtle suggestive ways. Not outright by saying, "pick this one; this guy, "but in ways far less conspicuous that are often unconscious even to the experimenter.

Once scientist realized that the experimenters were influencing the outcomes of their experiments. They developed what is known as the double blind experiment were the stimulus is administered by an uninvolved third party. Such as a police officer not involved in the case and who doesn't know who the suspect is.

Due to all the wrongful convictions around the country resulting from mistaken identifications, the Dallas Morning News ran an article on November 6, 1996 on mistaken identifications in which Forensic psychologist Dr. Kelly Goodness said, "The investigator showing the line-up should not know whether the suspect is in the photos because studies have shown that witnesses pick up on subtle cues."

For West, the stakes were high. He was on trial for a murder where the only evidence against him was the testimony of two witnesses. The common denominator in each identification was Detective Abby. He contacted the witnesses, he showed the witnesses the photo spread, and he recorded their identifications and levels of certainty. Yet since the process wasn't videotaped whatever happened or didn't happen during the process was a mystery.

Of course detective Abby testified that he didn't lead or make any suggestions to the witnesses. But it's doubtful that any homicide detective worth his salt would ever willing admit to such conduct, further more it ignores the essence of what the science of unconscious suggestion is all about.

So while the Houston Police department and the Harris County district attorney's office pretended to be ignorant of how the process worked, or of how it had contributed to wrongful convictions. U.S Supreme Court Justice William Brennan certainly wasn't in the case of U.S v. Wade he wrote, "The vagaries of eyewitness identification are well known the annals of Criminal law are rife with instances of mistaken identification. The trial which might determine the accused fate may well not be in the courtroom, but at the initial pretrial identification.

We do not assume that these risks are the result of police procedures intentionally designed to prejudice the accused. Rather we assume they derive from the dangers inherent in eyewitness identification and the suggestibility inherent in the context of pretrial identifications."

These were the issues the defendant and his attorney were concerned about, "the dangers inherent in eye witness identification and the suggestibility inherent in the context of pretrial identification," especially when everything was done by one police officer with no way of going back and reviewing the process.

Through the years, the issue has remained so problematic that the U.S. Justice Department conducted a study in 1999 and issued a report entitled "Eyewitness Evidence: A Guide for Law Enforcement." While the leading experts in the field, Dr. Gary Wells, Dr. Elizabeth Loftus and Dr. Stephen Penrod, have recommended the police adopt several procedures that would improve the process while simultaneously minimizing the number of mistaken identifications. Their recommendations are-that:

All lineups, photo spreads and other identification processes should be videotaped as this is the most important part of the entire process and often the only people present are the investigator and witness. Without recording the process, there is no conclusive way to reconstruct biasness, suggestiveness or hints.

Independent examiners should conduct the line up and photo spread. And the investigator should not know who the suspect is to prevent giving hints.

All witnesses should be asked to rate their degree or certainty during the time of the initial identification. Research has shown that once a witness makes a wrongful identification they are likely to persist in their identification and to become even more certain as time progresses. Often this results from them mentally reinforcing their own previous identification.

Police and prosecutors should be trained and warned against the risk of giving witnesses corroborating details as they are likely to show up in the witness's later recollections.

None of these best practices were observed in the defendant's case.

Baldassano tried to side step the fact that the identifications weren't obtained under the best possible circumstances or by using the best possible procedures.

Q: Before you showed him the photo spread, did you give the witness any kind of instruction?

A: Yes.

Q: And, what type of instruction did you give?

A: To look at the pictures carefully; that the photo spread itself may contain pictures of someone that was involved in the shooting.

Q: Did you ever suggest who to pick?

A: No

Q: Did you ever tell him that he had to pick somebody?

A: No.

Such questions tended to make good courtroom drama and they served the purpose of assuring the jury that everything was on the up and up. However, they didn't even scratch the surface of what Justice Brennan was talking about, of what suggestiveness was really about. The process was far from explicit, yet study after study has documented its existence.

Don Irvin took a few harmless swipes at detective Abby, but the shots were too wide, too short, or not hard enough. He did get him to admit that the other men in the victim's car didn't want to talk with him, behavior inconsistent with law abiding citizens who had just been the victims of a horrible crime. But detective Abby was a hard nut to crack. He had testified in numerous criminal trials and knew exactly what to say and what not to say.

Q: When you attempted to talk to them, were they ever uncooperative?

A: You mean throughout the investigation? To some degree, yes.

Q: Would you categorize them generally as uncooperative?

A: I wouldn't say generally; somewhat uncooperative?

Before detective Abby left the witness stand Don Irvin attempted to make a point concerning the photo spread, but lacked a scientific understanding of how to adequately raise the issue.

Q: And I believe when Mr. Baldassano was talking to you about I'll use the original as an example. You made a statement that what you did when you put a photo spread together to show to a potential witness is that you pick out pictures of people who look similar?

A: Yes.

Q: Can you tell me if number 6 looks similar to number 5?

A: Yes.

Q: Can you tell me if number 1 looks similar to number 5?

A: Yes.

When it comes to photo-based lineups there are two factors that can lead a witness to pick the wrong suspect. The first is what's called, "unfair bias," the second the "functional size" of the lineup. Experts in the field have developed techniques to check photo-based lineups for both of these phenomenon. In the average photo-based lineup, officers typically show witnesses six photos, one being a photo of the suspect. If the lineup is fair, the probability of a stranger who didn't witness the crime picking the suspect is one and six. As there are six potential choices.

With an unbiased lineup all non- witnesses who read a brief description of the suspect should only identify the suspect with a 1/6 probability because the only thing a non-witness has to go on is the brief description. In a fair unbiased photo-based lineup, all the suspects are supposed to look alike. Therefore, every person in a line-up has an equal chance of being picked and they should be picked at about the same rate by different non-witnesses acting on the description. If, however, the non-witnesses, based purely on the written description, consistently pick one person or photo more than the others, the lineup is unfair and the photos do not significantly resemble each other thus leading to a biased result - one individual being selected more than the others.

The second issue concerning photo based lineups is their functional size. This means that although a lineup might contain ten pictures, but three of the individuals look more alike than the others, i.e. they are all muscular and the suspect was said to be muscular, the functional size of the lineup is actually 3 not 10, leading the suspect to have a 1 out of 3 chance of being picked instead of 1 in 10.

These two issues, lineup biasness and functional size, are of upmost importance to criminal defendants. Research has shown that uncertain witness are likely to use extraneous information to strengthen their identifications, such as, "he was slim." Which means that a slim guy who happens to end up in a lineup with more beefy guys is likely on his way to prison, or worse.

These are the scientific grounds on which Don Irvin should've challenged the six person photo spread of the defendant. Not Detective Abby's opinion whether the pictures looked alike or not.[12]

The prosecution rest.

---

[12]A copy of the original photo spread has been reprinted in the exhibits section.

At the conclusion of Detective Abby's testimony, the state rested their case. Now the defense would have their chance to go on the offense. But they were getting off to a slow start.

In the ensuing days, they had encountered a series of roadblocks beginning with their witnesses. Initially, they had two witnesses scheduled to testify on the defendant's behalf: Tanika Robbins and Mario Bluitt.

Miss Bluitt was in the hallway ready to go, but Miss Robbins had disappeared. An all out effort was being made to locate her.

But an even larger storm was brewing at the defense table. The defendant was extremely dissatisfied with the quality of his legal representation. His gripe was he didn't believe Don Irvin was doing an effective job cross-examining the witnesses. He thought he was soft peddling. And by the time the state rested, the defendant was in a panic. He wanted the assistant counsel, E.J. Van Buren, to take over the cross-examinations and recall several witnesses to the stand beginning with Jessie Brown.

Jessie Brown worried him. He seemed believable when he testified that he saw the defendant from five to seven feet away discharging a gun had it not been for the fact that he knew he was mistaken. He probably would've believed him. His testimony bothered him and he wanted to get to the bottom of it. Did he really believe he saw him shooting? Was he just a convincing liar? Or, was it something else. Whatever it was, he wanted to find out and doubted if Don Irvin's easy going 'don't rock the boat' style was going to do it. Both attorneys vehemently disagreed with his desire to recall Jessie Brown to the witness stand to conduct what he called a 'real cross-examination,' since this disagreement was far from cordial. They sought to get it before the court.

Van Buren took the issue up with the court, "It's my opinion, personally, that the matters necessary for a proper and potentially successful jury argument have already been raised by Mr. Ervin's cross-examination. However, the defendant has stated, once again, that he wants that individual recalled. May I ask the defendant some questions on the record?"

Q: Mr. Ervin and I have both spoken with you about our feelings regarding that, and it's been both of our advice that you avoid that because it could be potentially harmful, correct?"

A: Yes.

Q: Knowing all that, is it still your desire that we recall Jessie Brown to the witness stand?

A: Yes.

The judge looked down exasperated; he didn't like the defendant fouling up the tight schedule he had set. "Mr. West, are you satisfied that you're a better lawyer than Mr. Ervin and Van Buren?

A: No, sir but I know what happened.

"Then why don't you take their advice?"The defendant stared at the judge incredulously. Was this judge sitting through the same trial he was? "Why don't I take their advice," he thought. For starters, they were selling him down the river. People were sitting less than ten feet from him saying he did something he didn't do and his lawyer was asking questions like, "could you have seen better if it was daylight?"

The judge allowed them a few minutes to confer with their client. Eventually they were able to persuade him not to recall Jessie Brown to the witness stand but the defendant wasn't happy about it. It was the third time he strongly disagreed with their legal advice. He had already let them convince him not to testify and that in the event of his conviction to allow the judge to sentence him as opposed to the jury.

Marlo Chandoly Bluitt

With duct-tape on the rift at the defense table, they called their first witness - 24 year old Marlo Chandoly Bluitt, a dark-skinned black woman dressed in a light blue business suit.

Miss Bluitt took the stand. She had gone to the Boxapoolaza concert before going to the Carrington Club. After the club closed, she was walking to her car parked in the back of the lot over by the Arby's accompanied by her friend Tiffany Pruitt. Tiffany was driving and Miss Bluitt said she was standing next to the passenger door when she heard a volley of gun fire. She ducked in the doorway of her car.

When the shooting stopped, she stood up and saw a guy she knew running toward her. Concerned for his safety, she hollered for him to get down. At that point she watched him stick a gun in his waist band. Then she saw two more guys with guns running behind him. Miss Bluitt knew the defendant and testified that he wasn't the guy she knew, or one of the other two guys she saw running with guns.

Van Buren asked her about the other two guys she saw with guns.

Q: Was Kenneth West either one of the individuals you saw running with guns?

A: No.

From the moment Miss Bluitt took the stand, Baldassano hated her. He stopped just short of accusing her of being a liar, and tried his best to rattle her. When that didn't work he started proposing wild theories about why she didn't see the defendant with a gun. Perhaps it was five guys shooting? Or maybe one of the shooters ran the opposite way? And maybe that one was the defendant?

Q: You didn't see how many guys did the shooting?

A: No.

Q: It could have been one person, it could have been five people as far as you know, right?

A: I seen three guys running.

Of course what Baldassano was proposing was impossible based on the evidence, but that was beside the point. In the end, he did a lot of hollering and accusing, but Miss Bluitt held her ground. She saw three guys with guns and the defendant Kenneth West wasn't one of them.

Right when the defense seemed to be shifting into gear they suffered another setback.

The bailiff had located Miss Robbins, the second witness scheduled to testify. But when Van Buren spoke to her over the phone, she suddenly developed a severe case of amnesia. Now she wasn't sure who or what she saw. For whatever reason she had decided to remove herself from the equation and a sudden foggy memory was the perfect way to do it.

Her testimony would've been extremely helpful to the defense. On the night of the shooting, she was in the Carrington's parking lot and was interviewed by Detective Vachris. She told the detective she looked toward the area where she thought the shots were fired and saw a chubby, black male with brown skin and a low hair cut. He was wearing a stripped white and blue shirt and white jeans and new Air Jordan basketball shoes. She said she saw this black male putting a black pistol in the waistband under his shirt as he ran through the parking lot toward main. She told the detective that this individual was followed by two other black males and that she could positively identify one of them.

A few days later, Detective Abbondondolo and Vachris travelled to Miss Robbins apartment and showed her a photo spread. At this time Miss Robbins positively identified the defendant Kenneth West as the chubby brown skinned man she had saw in the stripped blue and white shirt, white jeans and Air Jordan basketball shoes. This was a crucial piece of testimony because unless the defendant possessed the supernatural ability to change clothes in the blink of an eye, it was impossible for him to be one of the shooters Jessie Brown testified he saw who he was certain was wearing a blue or burgundy football jersey with white numbers.

Yet both Tanika Robbins and Jessie Brown were positive in their identifications and had given sworn statements to that effect. Miss Robbins was so positive that she could describe the tennis shoes the defendant was wearing and her recollection was given in the hours immediately after the shooting.

Baldassano had hinted at these inconsistencies in voir dire saying people see things differently, but not this differently. The only logical explanation was that they had seen two different individuals who possibly bore some resemblance.

But, without Miss Robbins' testimony, the defense was unable to raise these issues and was left with no choice but to rest.[13]

With that done, there was another matter the defense lawyers wanted to get on record outside the presence of the jury.

The defendant felt he was being sold-out and was demanding to be allowed to testify in his own defense. He felt that unless he took the stand and told the jury out of his own mouth that he didn't kill Sammie Ray Johnson, he didn't have a chance in hell of winning an acquittal.

Of course his lawyers didn't agree and they had been around the block enough to realize that in the event of his conviction, he was likely going to claim ineffective assistance of counsel; they wanted to protect themselves in advance.

First, they got the defendant to relent on his vocal desire to testify, and then Van Buren took him back on record. He told the court, "For the purpose of the record, we have previously conferred with the defendant and advised him of the ramifications of his possible testimony and it's his desire not to testify."

From then on, every time lawyer and client disagreed he got it on record. By doing so, he could, and would, later claim that any errors in his trial strategy were simply the result of following his client's wishes. It was equivalent to a doctor in a malpractice suit, arguing that he was negligent because of the patient's wishes.

---

[13] Miss Robbins original statement has been reprinted in Appendix 1

While the defense attorney's appeared to be doing a good job of looking out for their own interest, the same couldn't be said for the defendant's.

Such occurrences had been a regular phenomenon for E.J Van Buren. After the West trial, he was cited by the state bar for failing to keep his clients informed, as well as failing to explain legal matters to his clients.

The following year, he was back in trouble with the bar for neglecting a legal matter and failing to fulfill his obligation to clients. This time he had failed to appear nine times in a Montgomery County District Court on a client's behalf.

By 2004, the Bar had had enough of Van Buren's antics and he was disbarred for multiple rule violations involving his inadequate representation clients. But for the defendant, the Bar's actions were too little, too late.

With the jury still out of the courtroom Baldassano had a matter of his own that he wanted to take up with the court. The two defense attorneys joined the prosecutor at the bench and the defendant strained his ears to hear what they were discussing. The only word he could make out was, "extraneous offense," as it seemed to be the one most frequently in use.

When Don Irvin explained to him what it meant, he stared off into space. It was like a doctor telling a patient he had terminal cancer and thirty days to live. Things couldn't get much worse.

Now everything made sense to him. The reason Baldassano was so adamant about taking him to trial on this case first even though it happened nearly a year after the self-defense case and was by all accounts the weaker of the two.

When he looked up, his eyes fell on Baldassano and they followed the prosecutor around the courtroom. Up under the mop of curly hair and behind the charismatic smile was a cold, calculating Harris County prosecutor who would do anything to win, even if it meant convicting a innocent man.

Chapter Three - Extraneous Offense

The atmosphere in the courtroom had dramatically changed. Both defense attorneys appeared visibly shaken, maybe they expected this? If so neither had breathed a word to their client.

The defendant could feel the worried tension. Something big was about to happen, something that would make or break his fate.

Stressed, he disengaged and his mind wondered. Back in the tank, a few older convicts who had been through the system too many times to count warned him, "Man you gotta be crazy. Never go to trial in Harris County, innocent or not you can't win."

He had gotten upset with the older man, "You think I'm just gonna plea to something I didn't do, you crazy."

The old convict had two rotten teeth left and even fewer patches of hair, but his head wasn't empty. He looked at the young kid in front of him still smelling like McDonalds and in more trouble than his 19 year old mind could understand and shook his head, "you'll see youngster. They don't play fair."

Don Irvin's voice grabbed his attention as he explained to him again what an extraneous offense meant legally, but more specifically what it meant to him at the moment, minus the slang and broken English he was telling him the same thing the old convict had, "they don't play fair."

What the defendant understood was that he was screwed. An extraneous offense was another offense believed to be committed by the same individual. As applied to the defendant the extraneous offense was that he had been involved in a self- defense shooting eight months earlier across the street from the Carrington's Club at the Exxon station that had resulted in the death of 23 year old Efrem Breaux.

To Baldassano's way of thinking, that was proof of the defendant's guilt in the instant case notwithstanding that the two cases were nothing alike.

In the Exxon case, the defendant admitted that he was involved and had several witnesses prepared to testify that they saw the deceased pull a gun on him.

On paper, the courts had strict rules dealing with when and how such evidence could be admitted in a criminal proceeding. These rules of evidence were written to prevent abuses but more often than not, the rules written by the legislature said one thing, yet the actual practice of prosecutors was another. Often this was because prosecutors knew they could get away with it. Appeal courts in Texas are extremely conservative and rarely overturn cases even for just cause. Combine that with pro-prosecution, Republican judges who were more likely to rule in prosecutors favor than they were defense attorneys and a situation was created where a prosecutor in Harris County could basically do whatever he or she wanted to. No one would stop him. Not the judge who had to worry about re-election and couldn't afford to be seen as soft on crime, nor the conservative appeal courts. In a case a few years back, a female prosecutor had a bed brought into the courtroom, then a male prosecutor laid on the bed while she proceed to straddle him in a stimulated sexual position allegedly to demonstrate how a woman had killed her husband. In refusing to overturn the case, the appellant court found this to be a harmless error. Before that the same appeal courts ruled that an attorney who slept through a defendant's trial, didn't necessarily constitute an ineffective attorney.

The judge hadn't made his ruling yet, but when he did, it was likely to be for the prosecution. If he did allow evidence of the extraneous offense to be admitted into the guilt or innocence phase of the trial, the defendant would essentially be on trial for two murders at once.

Ray Charles could see the outcome of that. Jurors were human and no jury in its right mind would believe him now. His last hope was that the judge would be fair and allow each case to be tried on its merits, which was what justice called for. No more, no less.

Baldassano had other ideas and began making his case for the inclusion of the extraneous offense. He told the court, "We would seek to put on a rebuttal to explain motive and identification with an extraneous offense which occurred six months prior on the other side of the parking lot across the street at the Exxon station."[14]

West tried to get Don Irvin's attention. Baldassano was lying and it seemed to him he had been doing that ever so subtly throughout the trial. Just then, he had said six months, when the self-defense case had happened November 9, 1996 and the other on June 6, 1997 which was nearly eight months and the Exxon station was a block away from the Carrington club. Maybe the discrepancies were minor, but to the defendant everything mattered. But his lawyer waved him off, he was busy listening to the prosecutor. Who continued, "The state is allowed to prove in the case in chief, or in rebuttal, can prove intent, motive, opportunity, plan

[14]Back in Voir Dire the, "Motive" wasn't important to the prosecutor. According to Baldassano, it was something the state didn't have to prove. But now that it helped his argument concerning the extraneous, the prosecutor was suddenly interested proving motive.

and identify. And we would seek to prove motive that the same type of offense happened six months earlier and also the identity of this defendant."

The judge, a short round man with dark eyes, interjected, "But, the similarities aren't an issue unless identity is an issue. Would you agree?"

Baldassano agreed, "I believe identity is an issue because that really is the whole issue in the case, whether or not the defendant is a shooter."

Don Irvin made an argument against the admission of the extraneous in the guilt or innocent phase, but it seemed the judge had already made up his mind. He was still talking when the judge said, "I'm going to go ahead and let it in. The identity portion, I'm over that hurdle. Now we get to the 403 bit, the similarities."

Switching tactics, Don Irvin tried to appeal to the judge's sense of fairness and told him, "If this other case comes in and you try to prove two murders in one trial, this is no longer a contest. There is no longer a consideration, I don't think, in the jurors' mind, did he commit this crime—well, look; the police think he committed another crime out here like this. If we're not going to convict him for this one, we'll convict him for that one. I just can't plead with the court strongly enough based on the fairness and equity aspect of this, and on the idea that the prejudices here are so heavy, that the scales would tip completely over in terms of probative value of this to help prove he committed this crime. It's just not going to be a contest anymore."

While it was hard to tell exactly how much sway the argument had on the judge, for a few seconds he did rock back in his chair and seemed to be giving it some thought. After all, the judge's part in the trial was to be a neutral observer and to insure that the law as applicable was followed. If he allowed the extraneous, would he still be doing that or would he be guaranteeing the prosecution a conviction?

Seeing the judge's indecisiveness, Baldassano filled the silence, "We're not going to put on the whole case. We might put on one or two people in the car; and then Christopher St. Romain, the main I.D witness and the detective that worked the case, and maybe somebody that examined the car."

That was all Judge Burdette needed to hear, he was a product of the Harris County conviction machine and had to act accordingly. He raised his hands silencing the opposing attorneys and said, "I understand your concerns and your objections. I'm perfectly satisfied I do. I am however, going to admit it. Be ready at 9:00."

The court adjourned for the day and the bailiff escorted the defendant from the courtroom to the court transfer area where he was left to make the long, solitary walk back through the maze of underground tunnels leading to the main jail. By now the bulk of prisoners who had attended morning court appearances were already back in their cells. With the exception of the surveillance cameras monitoring his every move he was alone. And it was the loneliest, aloneness he had ever experienced. For it was an aloneness without hope and in that moment, he knew he was being railroaded. He never had a chance. The trial was a sham.

Sometime along the solitary trek, he was handed a cold bologna sandwich in a sandwich bag with two pieces of bread and a two ounce cup of mixed peanut butter, known as a court lunch, but it passed from his hand to the trash in one fluid motion.

Back in the tank, the other inmates were waiting on the latest news, “What happened?”

From the domino table someone asked, “How it go?”

The look on his face said it all and he headed straight for the phones attached to the wall. As if on cue, the rest of the prisoners left him alone, it was understood that things weren’t going well. And the unwritten rules of the jailhouse said that when that happened to just leave a guy alone. Give him space.

His mother was waiting on the call. She had just as much at stake as he did. Not only was she facing the prospect of losing her only son for only God knew how long, but in an effort to ensure that he had some kind of legal defense she depleted her entire retirement savings and when that wasn’t enough, she mortgaged her home. But still it wasn’t enough. She listened to the operator, “This is a collect call from the Harris County jail will you except?”

“Yes.”

“Momma, they missing over me,” were his first words.

“I know; pray about it, baby. Everything happens for a reason.”

A few minutes later, the operator was back on the line, “You have one minute left.”

She promised to see him tomorrow in court and that his sister and nephew would be there with her.

"Alright Momma; I love you."

"I love you too, don't worry."

When the call ended, not even bothering to get undressed, he climbed into bed pulled the grey wool blanket over his head and cried. Although he had been in the county jail a year awaiting his day in court, it was the first time he cried.

Chapter Four - No Contest

> *"We're supposed to have a system that guarantees justice for all, but that's not what we have. It's a system dedicated to getting convictions."*

Terry O'Rouke
Ex-assistant Harris County attorney.

August 6

The adversarial trial process dates back to England, but its' origins are even older, as early as Moses day, a bare bones form of trial by jury existed where an accused person got to face his or her accuser before the community. The soul of the process was truth; a search for the truth.

In our day and age, the simple idea of truth has been knocked off the throne of justice and a person's guilt or innocence often rested on factors that had nothing to do with this simple concept of truth. Such as the judge's rulings of what evidence to allow or not to allow, questionable maneuvers by the prosecutor, the quality of the defense attorney, which more often than not is related to the defendant's social-economic status, as well as his or her race. In light of these factors, guilt or innocence has been reduced to an after though.

That an American prosecutor who enters the courtroom with unlimited resources compared to the average defendant and the presumption of right on his side can convict an innocent person is no longer a question. The 230 DNA exonerations around the nation, as well as the 37 in Texas, alone have already provided an answer but the mechanics of wrongful convictions often remain unknown to the general public which led to situations where history continuously repeats itself.

When Don Irvin told the judge that if he allowed evidence of the extraneous murder to be admitted in the trial, it would no longer be a contest, he was telling him that from the time the judge allowed the jury to hear that the defendant was charged with another murder, he would be guilty regardless if the evidence in the instant case supported his guilty, regardless of the circumstances surrounding the other case.

Early on the morning of August 6, the state reopened their case to present evidence of the extraneous offense. If the defendant had any hope, it was that he had a strong self-defense claim backed-up by three eyewitnesses and supported by the state's own I.D witness. But would the jury be able to distinguish between the two cases?

In the case the defendant was on trial for, a man, Sammie Ray Johnson, was gunned down for no apparent reason. Several months after the shooting, two friends of the victim were found who subsequently identified the defendant as one of the three or four shooters they saw. But in the extraneous case, the defendant thought he saw several guys following him and, thinking it spelled trouble, he left and went across the street to the Exxon station. Here he was talking to friends when the same individuals arrived and somebody screamed, "They got a gun." After seeing a gun emerge from the window, the defendant drew his own gun and fired. Those were the facts, but would the jury care? In face of the magnitude of the allegations against him, would they be able to remain impartial and carefully weigh the evidence or would they simply see the defendant as someone who went to nightclubs and shot and killed innocent people for no apparent reason and therefore needed to be removed from society. It was the latter view of the defendant that Baldassano was no doubt hoping for.

Christopher St. Romain

Since the defendant had yet to be convicted of the death of Efrem Breaux, the charge was still an unproven allegation forcing the state to conduct a kind of mini-trial in the middle of the initial trial.

Baldassano began with Christopher St.Romain[15], a short obese man with a shaved head and gold teeth in his mouth. He started off a problematic witness for the state. He knew the defendant from the neighborhood and it was St. Romain, who was referred to as "Big Chris" by his friends, who the defendant had turned to in the Carrington's parking lot for help when he first became afraid that the guys he was later accused of shooting were following him.

St. Romain was also a notorious and unrepentant drug abuser with marijuana, PCP, codeine-based cough syrup and alcohol being his drugs of choice. Eventually, it was his drug addiction, coupled with his weight problem that claimed his life a few years later.

Dressed casually in khaki pants and stripped shirt, St. Romain took the stand and tried to avoid eye contact with his former friend. A lot of guys in the neighborhood had been giving him flack for his decision to testify against the defendant, who was generally well liked by most people who knew him. The defendant had never said anything bad about St. Romain.

---

[15]For several years after the West trial ended, St. Romain's drug problem continued to worsen leading to multiple stints in jail and prison. In 2006 at the age of 29, St. Romain passed.

For him, life had a devine plan, although that plan was often hidden from the individuals who had to live it.

Nevertheless the defendant wanted one thing from St. Romain and it was for him to tell the truth; only the truth. The truth needed no additives it was a force unto itself.

After telling the jury his name, Baldassano led St. Romain into the fact that he was high on numerous drugs on the night of November 9, when the shooting occurred.

Q: Before you got to the Carrington's Club, did you drink or do anything like that?

A: Yes Sir.

Q: And what did you do?

A: I smoked marijuana and drank syrup with codeine.

Q: And, did you have anything else other than what you mentioned?

A: I popped pills; some Xanaxes.

Q: Drink anything at the club?

A: I drunk a Bailey and Henessey.

After establishing the fact that he was thoroughly intoxicated, he went on to say that he went to the Carrington's Club at 12:00 or 12:30 with Jerome Bradford and they went inside the club. When the club closed, he was walking around the parking lot and the defendant Kenneth West approached him in a panic. The first words out his mouth to St. Romain was, "Walk with me," because he thought four guys were following him and acting like they wanted to do something to him. He believed that if the guys who had caught his attention were really up to something, they would probably reconsider now that he wasn't alone. And since Jerome Bradford had to return his mother's car, St. Romain opted to ride home with the defendant in a car occupied by Christopher White and Greg Winfree. While White was driving, Winfree was in the backseat sound asleep. As the foursome drove from the parking lot, the defendant told St. Romain that maybe he was just being paranoid due to the excessive amount of gold and diamond jewelry he had on. Not many people knew it, but the majority of it was costume, yet it was easy to assume he was wearing a small mint.

They were in traffic leaving the nightclub when White pointed to two fancy Chevy Tahoe trucks, a green one and a black one, parked at the edge of the Exxon parking lot. The two trucks belonged to Bubba and Pop, good friends of theirs and so they pulled over to talk with them. At the Exxon station, St. Romain testified that the defendant was talking to a guy named Top Dog while he was talking to a friend of his named Cerald Bell. They had been at the station for a few minutes when White, the defendant's co-defendant, noticed the guys from Carrington's parking lot pulling up and told the defendant, "There go those guys from the parking lot that were looking at you funny." The guys he was referring to were riding in a green Hyundai Elantra with chrome rims.

The defendant had already noticed the car when it first drove up even before White alerted him to it but didn't want to jump to conclusions. That the same guys would show up at the same station didn't necessarily mean anything. It was fairly common for club goers to hang out in the area surrounding the club up and down South Main after the club let out. Yet, what did strike him as odd was that the rear passenger window was down. Being early November, it was cold. No one was riding around that time of morning with their windows down.

After alerting West and St. Romain to the presence of the green Hyundai, St. Romain testified that White took it upon himself to ask the guys if they had any plex, street slang for beef.

Q: When Chris makes this statement, asks this question, did you see the guy in the back seat bend down?

A: He was like … yes, sir.

Q: Did you see him reaching toward the floorboard?

A: Floorboard?

Q: Okay, could you see from your position there whether he had a gun or not?

A: No, sir

Q: And, it was Chris that then said they've got a gun.

A: Yes, sir.

Q: And, you must have thought it might be true, is that correct?

A: Yes, sir. I took off running.

Q: Why would you think it might be true? Seeing what you saw there, what made you run?

..e said they got a gun. I don't have a gun on me. I took off running. He said it loud - they got a gun.

Q: And, in fact, did someone push you out of the way? One of them push you out of the way as you were starting to run?

A: Yes, sir.

Q: Who did that?

A: Kenneth pushed me.

Q: Now, Kenneth wouldn't just push you to hope that you fall down and hurt yourself, would he?

A: No, sir.

Q: Why do you think that Kenneth would push you?

A: Because the guys had a gun.[16]

In the end, St. Romain, the state's main witness, did more good than harm. He told the jury that the defendant was fearful some guys were out to rob him and they left the Carrington's parking lot to avoid a problem. Following their departure, the guys who the defendant was fearful of showed up across the street at the Exxon station where West and his party had gone to talk with friends. St. Romain also testified that he observed the deceased reaching toward the floorboard followed by White yelling, "They got a gun," forcefully enough to cause him to break and run. His testimony had established the defendant's self-defense claim, while illustrating how un-alike the Exxon case was from the one he was currently on trial for.

---

[16]According to the Texas Penal code 9.31(b), a person is justified in using force against another when and to the degree he reasonably believes the force is immediately necessary to protect himself against the other's use of unlawful force. Article 9.33. allows for the use of deadly force in protection of a third party.

Jacoric Alexander

Following St. Romain was 23 year old Jacoric Alexander, Efrem Breaux's cousin. On the night of Nov 9, they went to the Carrington's club with two friends, Jacobe and Dee. Their club outing was fairly uneventful. They had a few drinks, did a little mixing and left the club around 2:00 am. After leaving the club, Dee had to use the restroom and they stopped at the Exxon station. It was here, he said, they first encountered the defendant as they were pulling up to the gas pumps.

Although they were riding in Mr. Alexander's green Hyundai Elantra, Jacobe was driving and Alexander was in the passenger seat. Efrem and Dee were in the back seat with Mr. Breaux directly behind Alexander.

They were parked next to the gas pump waiting on Jacobe to return when Alexander said he noticed the defendant looking suspicious although he wasn't exactly sure what looked suspicious about him, he said, "I don't know. I looked at him at the time he was looking at the car rolling up. After that, I ain't paying no mind."

Then he testified that someone else approached his car and said something and the next thing he knew, he heard gunshots. At this point, his testimony became a bit fuzzy. After realizing they were being shot at, they raced from the parking lot and discovered that Efrem had been shot. However, they didn't drive to one of the numerous hospitals less than two miles down the street in the Medical center. Instead they drove away from the hospitals despite the fact that he was familiar with the area and knew where they were. He also testified that he didn't go to the police officers in front of the club for help, although he knew they were there also. Instead, they got on 610 freeway and drove for five or more minutes before flagging down a police officer on 59.

The defendant's attorney thought this was a little strange and asked him about it.

Q: What freeway did you get onto first?

A: 610

Q: And from 610, where did you go?

A: 59

Q: Did you ever get stopped before you got to the hospital?

A: I flagged the lawman down.

Q: Was it a marked unit?

A: Yeah.

Q: And where was that?

A: 610 and 59.

Q: About how long after the shooting at Exxon did you flag a police officer down?

A: About five minutes.

E.J. Van Buren paused and looked around at the jury like, do you guys believe this?

Q: Are you telling this jury that you went driving for a hospital, instead of driving right up Main to the hospital, you got on 610 to drive to 59 to find a hospital?

Alexander stuck to his story. Whatever they did that didn't make sense was simply the result of panic. Although his version of events was the opposite of the defendant's, his testimony was helpful to the defendant. He said he noticed the defendant when they "rolled up," looking suspicious. This was consistent with St. Romain's testimony that the guys the defendant pointed out to him in the Carrington's parking lot who he thought wanted to do something to him arrived at the Exxon after they did. And what Alexander took for suspicion on the defendant's part could've equally been interpreted as alarm upon seeing the same men from the parking lot pulled up at the Exxon. Alexander also conceded that he didn't know what his cousin Efrem was doing in the backseat or if he had let his window down.

Michael Wright, HPD Officer

The crime scene officer who examined Mr. Alexander's vehicle was 17 year police veteran Michael Wright. His testimony consisted of informing the jury that the car had been struck by multiple gunshots and that while searching the car, he didn't find any weapons.

Under cross-examination, the veteran police officer provided several doses of helpful information that corroborated the defendant's version of events. The first was that the back window in the car was down and that the men in the car had ample opportunity to get rid of a weapon on the five minute trek between South Main and 59. What made it so important was that the defense theory was that the guys in the green Elantra were after the defendant for one reason or another. When they couldn't get him in the club parking lot, they followed him across the street. And, that they had their rear window down shortly before the deceased pulled a gun which he pointed at the defendant and his friends, causing the defendant to act in self-defense. The challenge was proving their version of events.

Earlier Jacoric Alexander had been asked about the position of his car windows.

Q: Do you know if any of the windows in your car were up or down?

A: When we pulled in there, all of them was up because it was cold.

By using Officer Wright's testimony, Van Buren was able to prove from the physical evidence that Mr. Alexander was lying, either the back window was down or the back door was open.

Q: In defense 1, you see the trajectory of the bullet that hit the back of the seat, correct?

A: That is correct.

Q: Do you know where the entrance of that bullet was?

A: It is possible that the shot could have been made as is with this window in this position. That is to say, it could have entered if this window was down like this, through this opening. It also could have been made if this door had been open. Again, I wasn't at the scene so I don't know.

Q: So, in order for this shot to have placed the car in this condition, you would surmise that one of two things was probable out there. Would probably be a safe word?

A: Yes. I can't see any other way.

Q: That is, either the window was down or the door was open?

A: Correct.

Q: Now Mr. Baldassano stressed your exhaustive search of the vehicle for any possible weapons, anything that looked like any weapons, any knives, any pointed sticks, all that stuff. Who was in charge of searching the area between the Exxon and 610?

A: I have no idea sir; I was not at the scene.

Q: So, that would be a different witness than you that conducted the search along the roadway to see if a gun was discarded anywhere.

A: That's correct.

The defendant looked back at his mother, the look in his brown eyes saying, "I told you so. We got them in a lie; can't deny physical evidence." So far every witness the state presented had given creditability to his self-defense claim starting with St. Romain, Alexander had turned around and corroborated St. Romain's testimony by saying the defendant was looking suspicious when they, "rolled up," again proving that the defendant and his party hadn't followed them to the Exxon seeking a confrontation, but were already there talking with friends minding their business. Now the defense had succeeded in proving to the jury that although it was cold either the back window next to the deceased was down or the door was open. Furthermore, Alexander had lied and said it wasn't.

Though it was a dubious strategy fraught with moral decay as well as a complete disregard for justice, Baldassano was wise to do everything he could to keep from trying the Exxon case first. Standing alone with no tricks just witness for witness, it had "self-defense" written all over it. But, Baldassano recognized that he needed one case to get a conviction on the other without a conviction on one of them, he didn't stand a chance of winning a conviction against a defendant without a felony record based on the thin, unreliableness of his evidence. But, by combining the two and later threatening to do so, he could win convictions all day long.

The defense was being forced to defend the defendant against a case he wasn't on trial for. Baldassano's sole purpose of presenting testimony of the Exxon case was to inflame the jury and sway their verdict against the defendant in the murder of Sammie Ray Johnson.

When Baldassano pressed for the admission of the extraneous offense, there was little doubt that he was seeking what the U.S Supreme court called, "Unfair Prejudice" which the court defines as: "Prejudice which speaks to the capacity of some concededly relevant evidence to lure the fact-finder into declaring guilt on a ground different from proof to the offense charged. The risk that a jury will convict for crimes other than those charged, or that it will convict anyway because a bad person deserves punishment."

The jurors assembled in the 176th district courtroom were being asked the same thing - not if what happened at the Exxon was murder, knowing and intentionally taking the life of another without cause. The evidence said it wasn't. The question the DA raised in the juror's mind was "Is Kenneth West a bad person who deserves punishment?"

<u>Waymon Allen Jr., HPD Homicide SGT.</u>

Sgt. Allen was on duty on November 9, 1996 with his partner Roy Swenson when they responded to the Exxon call around five a.m. In lieu of going straight to the Exxon, they proceed to the location on 59 were the victims were with plans to go to the actual scene of the shooting later that morning. He testified that he first encountered the victims "close to the Galleria," which was "at least five or six miles from the Exxon station, if not more."

Since Baldassano had stressed to the jury that no guns were found in the victim's car E.J Van Buren was equally intent on proving to the jury there was a good reason for this and it wasn't that the men weren't armed.

Q: And, who was in charge - now, from the Exxon station there to 610, how far is that?

A: I would say it's a block, block and a half; not too far.

Q: Who searched that area?

A: Back to the - around the Loop?

Q: From the Exxon station to where you enter onto 610?

A: No one that I'm aware of.

Q: So if there was any guns or pointed sticks or knives or anything like that, no one was in charge of going to search and see if maybe they were along the roadway there having been discarded?

A: No, sir.

Q: And then from 610 to 59, that's an additional how many miles?

A: I would say its several miles; it's at least five or six miles.

Again the attorney was attempting to add credibility to the defense's assertion that the men in the green Hyundai were armed and that they likely got rid of their gun on the five to six mile drive from the Exxon station to the 5500 block of Southwest freeway where they flagged down a police officer.

This was important for the Exxon case, if the defendant could prove a gun was in the car, he could prove self-defense. However, the next point Van Buren tried to make using officer Allen's testimony went to the heart of the case the defendant was currently on trial for - the death of Sammie Ray Johnson. It was a crucial issue that detective C.P Abbondonolo had tapped danced around in an effort to avoid. The issue was how the defendant became a suspect in Mr. Johnson's murder to begin with. The defense was out to prove that once the defendant was a suspect in the unsolved Exxon shooting that occurred eight months before the murder of Sammie Ray Johnson. The Houston Police department was left with two unsolved cases on their hands. Since they already had two suspects in one case, once it was discovered that one of their suspects was in the Carrington's parking lot along with fifteen hundred other people on June 6. They began to focus exclusively on the defendant, excluding all other suspects and tailoring the details of the case to fit him. Such a scenario wasn't entirely farfetched. The defendant wasn't arrested or charged with either case until November of 1997, a year after the Exxon incident and four months after the other shooting. What the delay showed was from the word go, homicide detectives had serious problems with both cases and neither one was considered a slam-dunk. The police didn't wait a year in one case and four months in another to charge a suspect they knew was guilty, not if they had creditable evidence. Normally, an arrest is made within days of the initial incident.

This delay of arrest was more fire to the defense theory that the officers involved in the case played a more nefarious role than they were letting on. It seemed more than a little suspicious that out of fifteen hundred people in the Carrington's parking lot when Sammie Ray Johnson was killed, the only witnesses the detectives could find to say the defendant was the triggerman was two friends of the victim, who miraculously appeared two to three months after the shooting after Detective Abby found them with perfect memories of the shooting and the individuals who did it.

Under such circumstances, the defendant and his attorney had good reason to suspect foul play.

Instances of police becoming convinced of a suspect's guilt then misreading, or worse, twisting the facts of the case to fit that particular suspect were more common than most people would like to believe.

The heinous rape and murder of 7-year old Ashley Estell, as horrible as it is, offers a good illustration. Cute as a porcelain doll, Ashley went to a Plano Park with her parents to watch her older brother play soccer. While her parents were distracted, Ashley disappeared. When her frantic parents couldn't find her, the police and community kicked into high gear and made an exhaustive search of the area that included going door-to-door and handing out hundreds of fliers with the little girl's smiling face. They all hoped to bring the cute little girl, who had captured the hearts of her entire community, home safely to her worried sick parents.

Sadly, there wasn't a happy ending. The following day, Ashley's body was found. She had been raped and strangled to death. The salvage crime shocked the community … if children weren't safe with their parents?

Overnight, the spirit of friendship and community that had led complete strangers to canvas the city from one end to the other in search of the beautiful little girl turned to grief and anger. People were upset; they were mad and they wanted justice - justice for Ashley and justice for their own children who they saw in Ashley.

Senator Florence Shapiro of Plano got involved and authored a new set of stricter sex-offender laws that collectively became known as, "Ashley Laws."

Multiple detectives were assigned to the case, many who were fathers themselves and they vowed not to rest until the monster responsible for Ashley's senseless death was behind bars.

Into this picture entered convicted sex offender Michael Blair, after being publicly identified on the news and in the papers as a suspect. Three "eyewitnesses" stepped forward. They recognized Mr. Blair and had seen him at the park on the day Ashley was abducted. Neither of the witnesses had given any previous descriptions, or made any sketches of anyone prior to positively identifying Michael Blair. None of that mattered. The police had the break they were looking for. What was even better was the suspect fit the crime; Michael Blair was already a convicted child molester and since he had done it before, he was likely to have done it again this time.

From that moment forward any other suspects or persons of interest were forgotten. Michael Blair was the prime suspect. The police had their man and witnesses to prove it. With Blair in their sights, the detectives begin putting the pieces of Ashley's rape and murder together the way they thought they went.

A year later, in 1994 Michael Blair stood trial for the rape and murder of 7 year old Ashley Estelle. After 23 minutes of Delliberations, the jury decided that anyone who could commit such a horrible crime against a defenseless, innocent child deserved the ultimate punishment. Michael Blair would die in the Texas death chamber by lethal injection for his crime. He was a monster and unfit to live. Redemption was beyond him and prison was too good for him.

Collectively, the public breathed a sigh of relief - another predator was off the streets. The Plano DA, along with the selfless detectives who had donated countless hours to assuring that Ashley got the justice she deserved, figuratively patted each other on the back for a job well done. Michael Blair would never harm another child this side of heaven.

There was only one problem. Michael Blair was innocent. He didn't rape and kill 7 year old Ashley Estell. In 2008, DNA proved it and he became the ninth innocent person released from Texas's Death Row. When he dismissed the case, District Judge Grey Brewer said "It has been determined that the case should be dismissed in the interest of justice that the offense charged in the indictment can be further investigated."

What happened? Where did the system break down? How did so many educated, ethical, experienced and moral people get it wrong? How did an innocent man end up spending 14 years on death row waiting to die for a crime he didn't commit? While the real "monster" remained free to prey on other children. How does a man go from potentially being seen in an area, to a child rapist and murderer?

And how often does it happen? Even scarier what would've happened if there wasn't any DNA and Blair's conviction was based strictly on eyewitness testimony? Would an innocent man have been put to death for a crime he didn't commit? These are the questions the criminal justice system continuously refuses to answer but that fail to go away.

What happened to Michael Blair happened because eyewitnesses make mistakes; police officers make mistakes and the criminal justice system puts a premium on winning convictions at the expense of justice.

It happened because Mr. Blair wasn't a sympathetic figure, he was already a convicted sex offender, a person most people considered the scum of the earth, who doesn't deserve even the minimum vestiges of justice. But, was the defendant Kenneth West much different? Where did society draw the line? Who deserves justice and who doesn't? Who deserves a fair trial and who doesn't? Did the fact that he had been involved in another shooting mean he didn't deserve a fair trial or the same standard of justice as Tom Delay, Martha Steward, Robert Durst or Ken Lay? Baldassano and Judge Burdette didn't think so. They would likely argue that wrongful convictions were isolated incidents; after all, the Blair case happened in Plano. Yet, Ronald Taylor, Joshua Sutton, Alex Pena and Richardo Rachel would disagree, they were wrongfully convicted in Harris County and there are an estimated eight-thousand wrongfully conviction in the United States every year.

But Baldassano was out to convince the jury that it didn't happen this time. Everything was legit - textbook perfect.

Q: Did that come to pass that you talked to him (Detective Abby) about that case?

A: Well, it resulted as a result of me developing my case. I was aware that officer Abbondondolo was investigating this homicide, that they both occurred in close proximity to the Carrington nightclub and that a 9-millimeter weapon had also been used in his case. So we shared information in an effort to develop the defendants.

Figuring this was satisfactory, Baldassano moved on; he needed to tackle another important issue as there was one detail that could be considered to exonerate the defendant and knowing the defense was dying to introduce it to the jury, he was intent on stealing their thunder. If he waited and let the defense bring it up, they would harp on it as the big deal it was. But, if he brought it up, he could always come back and tell the jury "Aw shucks; that's nothing. Remember? We told you that."

Q: And, did you ever have the bullets that you collected, or were collected in your case, compared to the bullets that were collected in his case?

A: Yes.

Q: Compared to each other?

A: Yes, I did.

Q: And, it turned out that the bullets, as far as that comparison went, did not come from the same guns? Is that safe to say?

A: Yes, sir; the same weapons were not used.

Different guns; no big deal. Now let's move on was Baldassano's attitude but it was a big deal. The defendant was 18 years old at the time of these shootings, not old enough to legally drink much less purchase a handgun.

Yet, with two guns fired in one incident and three in the other, the defendant would've had to have access to at least five different handguns on two separate occasions.

If 18 year olds in Houston had access to such arsenals, to where they could cycle through multiple illegal handguns, then it was understandable why Houston consistently had one of the highest murder rates in the country.

Under cross examination Van Buren led Detective Allen back to the issue of different guns and the part he personally played in the Sammie Johnson case.

Q: Now, going to the tying of these two cases, or the attempt to, the first thing you do is you want to see if maybe you've got the same weapon, was the same gun used? Is that right? Or guns?

A: Yes, sir. I had asked that comparison be made to those guns. I believe that was in June or July of 97 and I was trying to establish whether the same firearm could have possibly been used, even though a few months had lapsed.

Q: And, you find out that the answer is no?

A: That's correct.

Q: But, still do you suggest to officer A, if I may, that he put Kenneth West's picture in his photo line-up that he's taking around to people?

A: No, sir - well, you say suggest. I think that that decision was made because at the time, the vehicle being driven by Kenneth West, that license plate was captured at the scene of the homicide in his case.

Q: That car had been there at the scene at the Carrington Club that morning; was that correct?

A: That's what I was told; yes, sir.

Q: And, at that point, you had no witnesses or did you know of any witnesses that had come forth and identified Kenneth West as being involved in that particular case? Did he have any witnesses that you knew of?

A: I knew he had witnesses but up until I took a photograph of Kenneth, he didn't have a photo.

Q: So, you took a photo of Kenneth and said "Why don't you take this photo to the witnesses and see if maybe they identify him as being there. He had his car there that night and we have him in this case?"

A: No, sir. At that particular point in time, he was still just a suspect in my case. I didn't have him in my case or he wasn't charged in my case. We were developing the two.

Sgt. Allen mentioning that he thought the license plate of the defendant's car had been captured was the first time the information had ever entered into record.

While the defendant admitted he was in the parking lot, the sudden revelation about the defendant's license plate allegedly being captured didn't add up. According to the detectives, an anonymous witness had approached an officer and given him a description of the defendant's vehicle along with the license plate number. But for some reason, the officer never got the witness's name, phone number or any other identifying information. That any experienced police officer would let a material witnesses to a murder vanish without so much as a phone number is highly unlikely, not to mention against policy.

Yet, that was the detective's story and the defense could take it or leave it; but one thing they couldn't do was challenge it.

Recognizing that the mysterious witness story was a bit flimsy, while on the witness stand Detective Abby had conspicuously failed to mention it. Why?

If some witness had written down the defendant's license plate, his or her testimony could've been extremely helpful to the defense as it could've been used to prove that the defendant was alone on the night Sammie Ray Johnson was killed and not with two or three co-defendants as the prosecutor had said.

Up until this moment, Van Buren had done a fairly good job cross-examining Sgt. Allen. But at this point, he dropped the ball and his poor trial preparation manifested itself. It turned out there was a surveillance tape from the Exxon, but neither the defendant nor his attorney had ever viewed its contents and as a result, they were left to accept Detective Allen's explanation of what the tape showed or didn't show.

Q: The surveillance tape that you obtained from the Exxon, did it depict the parking area where the gas pumps were located?

A: Just the central pumps. Unfortunately the camera was not functioning properly and the actual shooting itself is not captured on the tape.

If the tape didn't show the actual shooting, what did it show? Had it been erased or altered? And, with the evidence indicating that the Exxon station was extremely crowded in the moments preceding the shooting, could other witnesses have been identified using the surveillance tape?

It was Van Buren's responsibility to get answers to these questions, but he never did. As a result, they remain unanswered.

Sgt Allen was the state's last witness concerning the extraneous offense and with the conclusion of his testimony the state rested for the second time.

The Exxon case had holes in it, perhaps it was self-defense. None of that mattered. That was for another jury to decide. Baldassano simply wanted this jury to know the defendant had shot a man a year earlier and therefore didn't deserve the benefit of the doubt.

If the jury couldn't convict him in the death of Sammie Ray Johnson based purely on the flaky testimony of the victim's two friends, surly they could now after learning of the extraneous offense. A gambling man would wager that the twelve people who were the exclusive judges of the defendant's fate had already made up their minds about his guilt or innocence and he'd probably be right - more than likely the defendant was on his way to prison.

<u>The Defense</u>

For most people just knowing about the extraneous murder was overwhelming regardless of the circumstances involved. It was like knowing Michael Blair was already a convicted child molester when he was subsequently charged with raping and murdering 7 year old Ashley Estelle. The police believed he did it. And, if he didn't, then who did?

That was the burden the defendant was facing, though it probably wouldn't matter, in the Exxon case, the defendant had a strong self-defense claim supported by several witnesses. He also planned to take the stand in his defense.

Although they didn't have to, they opted to put on a portion of their defense case in rebuttal to Baldassano's over all assertion that the defendant was a deranged 18 year old who went around killing people at nightclubs for the hell of it.

A conspicuous note taker throughout the trial, who could be seen whispering back and forth with his attorneys, West adjusted his silk tie while the first defense witness approached the stand.

Exactly how much hope he still possessed was hard to tell. Prior to the admission of the extraneous offense, he had remained optimistic even though things weren't going as well as he initially expected they would.

One thing he couldn't have known or expected at the time was that the current defense he was about to mount in the Exxon case, a defense to a case he wasn't on trial for, was the only defense he would ever be allowed to make in the case.

<u>Alvando Ray - Top Dog</u>

West and Ray were from the same part of Southeast Houston and had a casual relationship. Ray was in the Exxon parking lot the night of the shooting and he recalled that he was on his way to the store when he noticed four guys in a small green car parked by the gas pumps who looked suspicious to him.

Prior to noticing the gentlemen in the green Hyundai, he had finished holding a conversation with the defendant Kenneth West over by Buffalo Speedway. Van Buren asked him about this:

Q: Did you walk up to him or wave to him or anything like that?

A: Yeah, we said a few words to each other.

Q: Was he in a good mood or was he friendly to you?

A: He was always in a good mood.

Baldassano gave Mr. Ray a look of pure venom. Far as he was concerned, Alvando Ray was the defense witness from hell. His testimony was nearly an exact opposite of the prosecutor's lead witness Jacoric Alexander. Alexander had testified:

A: I seen that guy right there.

Q: Okay, had you ever seen him before?

A: No.

Q: When you saw him, what did you see him do?

A: Walking around looking like he was going to do something.

Q: When you say walking around, was he walking in front of your car or to the back of, or to the side.

A: I seen him on the side of my right.

Q: When you say he looked like he wanted to do something, can you elaborate? What exactly or you talking about?

A: Looking for trouble or something.

Q: Why do you say that?

A: That's how he looked … high or something … looking around.

Nevertheless Alvando Ray seemed to have seen the same thing that Alexander did, the only difference was the strange behavior he observed was coming from Mr. Alexander and his three friends. Mr.Ray also saw the deceased with a gun.

Q: What did you see?

A: I saw four guys in a car looking strange, like they was up to something.

Q: Okay, where was Kenneth at that time?

A: The last I saw him, he was over toward Buffalo Speedway.

Q: Okay. As you were walking towards the entrance, did anything unusual happen?

A: That's when I saw the guys in the car, right here parked next to the pump.

Q: Were their windows up or their windows down? Do you remember?

A: Yes, the windows had to be down because when I was walking toward the entrance, that's when I saw the guy in the back seat behind the passenger reach for something and then he stuck a black gun out of the window and I heard somebody say "Hey, they got a gun" and the next thing I know, somebody started shooting and everybody just started running everywhere.

Baldassano couldn't wait to cross-examine Mr. Ray. The man had nearly destroyed his conviction proof case and he ripped into him with everything he could muster. But Ray refused to be cowered; he had seen what he saw and that was that.

Frustrated that a truth existed other than the one he conceived in his mind, Baldassano turned to sarcasm.

Q: It was a good thing that you were watching, wasn't it, because those four guys, one of them happened to have a gun and you just spotted that ahead of time, right?

A: I mean, you know, some things you can just see.

Q: You're like a detective almost, right?

<u>Cerald Bell</u>

Twenty-one year old Cerald Bell's testimony wasn't as explosive as Ray's. He knew the defendant from school and was also in the Exxon parking lot the night of the shooting. He didn't see any guns, the shooting or who did it, but he did hear someone scream "They got a gun," followed by a lot of gunfire. Therefore, his testimony validated St. Romain's and Ray's, essentially there was some type of confrontation between the defendant's party and the men in the green Hyundai that lead to White screaming "They got a gun."

One interesting wrinkle of Mr. Bell's testimony was that he was riding with his friend Bubba in a fancy Chevy Tahoe. Bubba's Tahoe was parked next to Pop's Green Chevy Tahoe. These guys often rode behind each other. At first, it was believed that Bubba's truck was hit, but was later discovered that it was Pop's instead that was shot in the front grill. What was interesting was that Pop's truck was parked directly behind the green Hyundai about ten feet away. When the back seat passenger in the Hyundai pulled his gun, once the shooting started, the driver jumped out of the car and then hopped back inside. Yet it all happened so fast, no one was sure if he also had a gun that he tried to discharge. For that reason, the defense was scrambling to get Pop to court, as they were trying to determine if the single shot that hit Pop's front grill was fired by one of the men in the green Hyundai.

The Defense Rest

Chapter Five - Closing Arguments

The next morning, all the parties were assembled in the 176th District Courtroom for the final leg of the trial, closing arguments. Once the court gave the -jury the official charge, from then on, the defendant's fate would rest with the jury.

Before that could get under way, a quick hearing was held outside the presence of the jury.

The Court: All right. Prior to the time the charge as been read to the jury, Mr. Ervin representing the defendant, Kenneth West, has filed a special requested charge that heretofore has not been contained within the charge that was discussed yesterday relating to the request that I instruct the jury on the issue of self-defense on the extraneous offense.

Mr. Ervin: That's correct, Your Honor.

The Court: Anything in support of that?

Mr. Ervin: The reason it occurs to me to ask that, Judge, is that the jury will be asked to determine whether they can believe beyond a reasonable doubt the extraneous offense in determining whether or not an offense was committed. It seems to me, they would have to consider the affirmative defense that was advanced through the testimony and that's where it is self defense.

The Court: All right, sir. That request is denied. Bring in the jury.

Short and sweet, pro-prosecution, Republican judge through and through.

In Texas, the prosecutor was allowed to give two closing arguments compared to the defense's one. The order was the state, represented by its prosecutor, went first and gave the initial statement. The defense followed and then the state got another bite of the apple.

This didn't seem right to the defendant and he wondered who had thought up such a system. To him, it was like saying they got to punch him twice to his one punch and that was fair.

Closing arguments always promised lots of excitement and it wasn't uncommon to see attorneys dropping by to hear certain famed attorney's closing arguments as defense lawyers and prosecutors tended to use their closing arguments to practice a kind of high-flown oratory that often bordered on the theatrical.

With this in mind, twenty-four eyes were on Baldassano as he stood in the middle of the court room, "Please the court, defense counsel and members of the jury, first of all, I want to thank you for your time and attention. I know it's hard and everybody paid real close attention and that's important for both sides. Everybody on the jury suppressed the urge to reach out and strangle the lawyers when you maybe felt like doing it. Anyway, both sides appreciate your time and attention.

I want to go over some of the things the Judge mentioned in his jury charge, and some of the things the Judge, defense counsel and I talked about on jury selection. First of all, the jury charge is the law from the Judge. He's already told you that, and just to maybe simply go through it, it gives you what the Penal Code's definition of murder is. Basically, I intend to kill somebody and then kill them, or intend to cause serious bodily injury and they die. That's the definition of murder and the other legal definitions given, firearm, deadly weapon, and things like that. Then, it talks about parties, an accomplice or get-away driver. If a person aids, encourages, or attempts to aid, then that person is just as guilty as the person who did it. Like, again, the get-away driver. And, that's explained here, the general definition of party as it appears in the Penal Code. And then, what happens is, the Judge applies the law from the Penal Code to the facts of this case. That is intermingled with the law of murder. In Harris County, Texas, on or about June 6, 1997, this defendant killed Sammy Johnson, Jr., or Sammie Ray Johnson.

And so, that is the application part of it, and what the Judge does is apply the law of murder, just regular murder, intent to kill, to this case, and then applies the law of murder, intent to kill, with the party, that is, being an accomplice, intending to kill, to this case. And, that's on the middle of the second page. And, then the Judge does the same thing with the intent to cause serious bodily jury. That the defendant either did it directly, or he did it as a party. The reason I want to stress this is I want everybody to understand, and I think it really is common sense, that the Penal Code reflects that we don't have to prove whose bullet killed Sammy Ray Johnson, Jr. That would be virtually impossible, if all the defendant had to do is throw the gun away; the law reflects that. You can see here all you would have to believe is beyond a reasonable doubt this defendant acted with an unknown person or Christopher White to either kill or intend to cause serious bodily injury. It doesn't matter whose bullet entered the brain of Sammie Ray Johnson. It just simply doesn't matter. If you believe that, you should find him guilty. Those are the four ways the Judge talks about and applies the law to the facts. There are really four different alternatives that you have.

I want to talk briefly about beyond a reasonable doubt because it was dealt with at length on voir dire by the defense, and it's in the charge, and its part of the law. But, I also want to call your attention to the fact that in the definition they talk about common sense and, I think that's why we have jurors and that's why we have members of the community come in. The golden thread throughout the whole criminal justice system should be using common sense. I know by just the people's responses on the jury panel, you don't get the idea it's some impossible burden and it can never be met and you get kind of swamped in that whole legal definition without considering that it says use your common sense in the definition. It's a standard that's used in the country and everybody that's in prison in the country is there beyond a reasonable doubt. It's certainly not an impossible standard. And, the Judge does mention, in the most important of your own affairs. I would suggest to you that this is one of the most important of your own affairs. Even if you live out by the Carrington Club, or just as a member of the community, basically just using your common sense, you are reasonable people, and if you think the defendant is guilty, you should find him guilty. I think beyond a reasonable doubt, to me, is easier to explain in circumstantial evidence where you are following some kind of puzzle and trying to fit the pieces together to see if they work, or they leave a trail. But, here, you have eye witness direct testimony, and it's basically if you are going to believe the witnesses or not.

I want to talk a little bit about the extraneous the Judge mentioned when he talked about this in the jury charge, and the law. Who killed Sammie Ray Johnson. That's what the case is about. You can believe the extraneous if you want to, but you don't have to, to find the defendant guilty of killing Sammie Ray Johnson. It could help you, if it does, in considering the identity or something like that. We don't have to prove two murders. You can simply find this defendant guilty of killing Sammie Ray Johnson based on the evidence you heard independent of that earlier murder.

We talked a little about, I did, about the attorney's questions are not evidence. If I did it, it's not evidence, and if they did it, it's not evidence. Mr. Van Buren asking questions about the car being shot up or things like that, to be evidence, you need somebody with personal knowledge that knows what happened or a picture of the car, maybe the insurance company paperwork on the car being shot. And, the guy who's apparently a friend of all of these people coming in and saying yeah, my car was shot that night, something like that. But, repeating things over and over in the attorney's words, if I did it or they did it, or simply saying something, an attorney talking, that's not evidence in the case.

I talked briefly about description versus recognition in jury selection. We did the demonstration with the bailiff where I stood over here and I picked an unwilling volunteer and we talked about that. I think everybody knows the way our brain works. It's much easier to recognize somebody than to describe them. I think that goes without saying. You may not remember what kind of suit I was wearing yesterday, if it was tan or blue or gray or what, but you know I was here.

You might not remember everything I had on, and you saw me for several hours. I know you were here. I don't know what you were wearing, but I know you were here. That's just common sense. I don't need to belabor that.

One thing the defense attorney will talk to you for a while, and I think you can tell from any attorney, the degree to which they attack a witness is the degree to which they believe the witness hurt their case. And, they will attack witnesses. You have to look at the evidence as a whole, and just consider what the witnesses said. That's the evidence in the case. I suggest to you with a good lawyer, it's kind of tough to win as a witness. You were either too close in, in which case you were too afraid, and you couldn't possibly remember because you were running for your life, or you are too far away and you can't see. It's light out there, but it's not as light as day. If it's as light as day, it's certainly not as light as this courtroom. If it's as light as the courtroom, it's certainly not as light as something else; it kind of goes on and on. You look through that and think back to the testimony in the case. One thing about our witnesses, if their testimony is too similar, typically the defense says they got together and cooked up the story, conspired because they wanted to get their guy. If their stores are somewhat different, it's they are lying. They don't remember. I think the Judge says it best. I can take 50 of you in back of the courthouse, and you see something happen, and I bring all 50 of you back, and you have 50 different stores. That's the way the brain is. Everybody is not positively the same on every detail, especially as time goes by. It's different recognizing somebody you've seen to remembering where everybody was standing relative to everything else. Also, you look to the physical evidence. That will help you.

The defense attorney will talk to you, and I will have a chance to talk to you one other time. Again, I appreciate your time.

His motto was kill 'em with kindness and with that, Baldassano took his seat.

Don Irvin rose to his full height of nearly six feet. One thing no one could deny concerning Don Irvin was his impeccable sense of style. He was habitably dressed to the nines, from his tailor made shirts and earth-tone suits, down to the platinum submarine Rolex that accented his fleshly wrist. Of the three lawyers involved in the trial, Steve Baldassano, E.J. Van Buren and Don Irvin, Baldassano and Van Buren probably had the most in common; both possessed a common man, folksy sort of style. Don Irvin was the opposite; he came across as elite and scholarly without a desire to be any different.

Whether his erudite style would resonate with the jurors or not had yet to be seen. Standing before the small wood railing that separated him from the jurors he spoke in a clear concise voice, "Your Honor, Mr. Baldassano, ladies and gentlemen, the prosecutor has reserved the right to close the argument in this case. What that means is he gets to talk to you last. And I sort of have to anticipate what he's going to say. Remember this though, regardless of what he has to say to you about where the buck stops, how much money, time and effort was expended by the State in prosecuting Mr. West in this case, what you are going to say to your friends and your relatives about your verdict in this case, what message you are going to send to the community by your verdict in this case, that there is really only one question before you now and that is you, and only you individually, must decide whether you can be certain beyond a reasonable doubt that Kenneth West committed the offense that he's charged with here. If you can't do that, if you have a reasonable doubt, then you must, under your oath as jurors, and under the law, find him not guilty. I don't know how you people feel about this, but the service that you have been performing this week is a very important service. George Washington, who was the first commander-in-chief of our armed forces, the first President of the United States, the father of our country, once, said that the most important service that he ever performed for his country was serving on a jury. Why is that so important? It's important because our jury system distinguishes itself from other countries and makes us what we are. In other countries in the world, a police officer can go out on the street and point his finger at a person like Kenneth West and say, come with me, snatch him up, grab him, sit him down in a courtroom like that and say, okay, prove to us that you are innocent. That's not the way we do things in this country because in this country, the people are more important than the government. We say to the government, if you snatch one of us up and bring them into a courtroom like this and sit them down and sit us down, then you better be able to prove guilt, and you better be able to prove it beyond a reasonable doubt.

And, what is proof beyond a reasonable doubt? The court has instructed you proof beyond a reasonable doubt is proof of such a convincing character that you would be willing to rely and act upon it in the most important of your own affairs. Proof of such a convincing character that you would be willing to rely and act upon it without hesitation in the most important of your own affairs.

Imagine what the most important of your own affairs are, affairs dealing with the health of yourself and your family, affairs dealing with the security of yourself and your family. And, then imagine acting on that proof without hesitation, acting in those affairs without hesitation and you begin to get an idea of what proof beyond a reasonable doubt is. Proof beyond a reasonable doubt is the most precious legacy that Americans enjoy.

Let's examine the evidence in this case in light of that standard. The first thing I would like to talk to you about is the scene out there. I know you have heard a lot about this, and I don't want to beat a dead horse, but it's important you get a feeling for the scene, and there is a lot of confusing evidence what it's like out there. You are probably not confused, but I want to go through it with you anyway because the witnesses testified from this framework. There was a lot of testimony about lighting and I don't know if you remember the first witness for the State was Officer Stevens. And, she was asked the question by Mr. Baldassano, well, the lighting out there was worse than it is on the average street. She says, no, it wasn't - or, yes it was worse. I can't remember how it wasn't, but her testimony was to the effect that the lighting in the parking lot was worse than the average lighting on the average street.

I think probably the best thing to look at in terms of what the scene was like out there, in terms of the lighting, are the pictures that were introduced by the officer. I cross examined him, asking what ASA film he used to take the pictures, because the pictures were grainy. Look at those pictures. Even though they were taken with 400 ASA film, you still see substantial shadow and the light was dim. It wasn't bright. You heard a number of witnesses say I could have seen it a lot better if it were daylight. You have a marginal lighting situation. It's chaotic out there. I think you probably have a pretty good idea of this, but there are 1000 to 1500 people in the parking lot. There are cars with people in them, empty cars, people trying to get out of the parking lot. No one can move; the streets all around the parking lot, the traffic is blocked. You have people stranded, as Mr. Fields and Miss Gravett, in the area for a long period of time, sitting there. So, you have a very chaotic situation with crowds and crowds of people. Lots of people out there in a small area. Of course, everybody was partying out there, but nobody was drinking.

Now, one of the things I want to make sure you understand is we are not contesting that Kenneth West was out there that evening in that parking lot. What we are contesting is the State's theory that he was a shooter in this case, that he shot the car of Jerome Sampson. But, we are not contesting the fact that he was out there that night.

Now, the State brings you three witnesses that they want to use to convince you that Kenneth West was shooting out there that night, that he shot Jerome Sampson's car.

Now, the first one is Mr. Fields, whose testimony is kind of incredible. Even though he doesn't say he saw Kenneth West shooting, the situation, the area where he puts Kenneth West is something that the prosecution wants to make you feel like would make it more likely Kenneth West was actually the shooter.

Mr. Fields, if you remember, is the person who was in the automobile with his girlfriend in the intersection that's in front of Jerome Sampson's car, sitting there at the light. And, his testimony is that Tracy Gravett, who was driving the car, discovers that shooting is going on and says, oh my God, there is shooting, at which time - and these are the critical seconds - Mr. Fields looked over into all of this chaos for what he says are a couple of seconds and says that he sees Kenneth West in a position, that you remember he testified to, back behind the car there, that he identifies Kenneth West in a couple of seconds, the panic of oh, my God, they are shooting and everything.

At this point, he's in his chair, he tries to lean back and put his seat back so he can lay down and be out of the range of the shooting. Well, he can't do that, so he comes over and leans down on the seat over his girlfriend, until the shooting stops, and then he hears .... in other words, all of this time he's not looking down where Kenneth West is .... then he hears the car coming across the intersection ... Jerome Sampson's car coming across the intersection. And, he looks up and sees the car ... is not looking for Kenneth West at this time ... and the car slams into him, the left front fender, spins the car around, the car jumps the curb and lands with the back of the car that Mr. Fields was in facing the direction where the shooting was coming from.

So, you've got two seconds here, a couple of seconds here where Mr. Fields says that he's looking down into this chaos and recognizes Kenneth West among these other 1000 to 1500 people. And what makes it even more incredible is that he's nearsighted and doesn't have his glasses on. Of course, he admitted that he could have seen better with them on, which, of course, he could have.

Now, what makes his testimony more incredible is that he has an opportunity to tell the police officer out there at the scene, because he actually does talk to a police officer, I looked down there and I saw who was shooting. But, he doesn't do that in that interview. It's not until later that a police officer interviews him and shows him this photo spread that you have seen in evidence of what the officer testified to as similar-looking individuals. Well, look at the photo spread and decide for yourself whether or not they are similar. The only two people that look alike in that photo spread are Kenneth West and Christopher White. But, he sees this photo spread, something happens and he decides, well, that night, under those extraordinary circumstances, I saw Kenneth West, and he was in this position. I don't believe that his testimony convinces, beyond a reasonable doubt us, of anything.

There are only two witnesses in this case that say that they saw Kenneth West shooting. And, these two witnesses are friends. They rode to the parking lot and away from the parking lot with each other. They are both friends of Sammie Johnson, the individual who was killed in the car. And, they are also friends with some of the other people who were in the car also, and who were wounded. And, I want to talk to you about their testimony together because I don't feel like it's an accident that these two friends, who are also friends of the complainant in this case, and who--Mr. Risher, one of them--says he's familiar with Kenneth West--I don't feel it's an accident that these are the only two people out of the crowd of 1000 to 1500 people who identified Kenneth West as the shooter in this case, put a blazing gun in the hands of Kenneth West. Their testimony is incredible. They saw people; their testimony is they saw people who murdered their friend. This is different from witnesses who come in who have no involvement in the case personally, who don't know the person who died, who didn't witness the shooting. You have to consider the involvement of the individual with the incident itself before you determine whether or not they should or should not be forthcoming, or whether or not it comports with human logic that they would be forthcoming with information like this. But, instead of going to the police and saying, I saw who did this--and in Risher's case, I know Kenneth West and Kenneth West is the one who did this--they never go to the police and mention anything about this. The police have to approach them.

But, I think the most important thing, or one of the most important things for you to consider about both of their testimony is that they both got on the witness stand and told you that out there at the scene where they both witnessed a friend of theirs, who Brown said he loved, who Brown said he held in his lap while he was dying, that they witnessed this extraordinary thing and they both got in the car together and left the scene and didn't discuss it. Now, you know that's not true. That doesn't happen in real life. You witness the murder of your friend and you take off before you ever talk to the police or anything like that, jump in the car, you spend half an hour driving home, and you don't even talk about it. What this tells you is that these two men are capable of lying because that wasn't the truth. If that's not the truth, then especially under the circumstances and the logic of all of this, there are a lot of other things that are not the truth.

I don't know what happened here; don't understand what's going on here.

My inclination is to believe that because of the fact that they know each other, they were there with each other, they know the complainant in the case, they know the dead man, one of them says he knows Kenneth West, and they are the only ones in a crowd of 1000 to 1500 people, that somehow they cooked something up to accuse Kenneth West in this case. I don't know about that. I can't prove that. But, I guess since they never have talked to each other about the crime, they couldn't have cooked something up, so I don't know. I think that these facts alone create a reasonable doubt as to their testimony.

Just the facts that I have related about their testimony creates reasonable doubt, but their testimony gets worse than that. Mr. Risher, when he testifies, says he doesn't remember anything about color or anything about the clothes that he says Kenneth West was wearing out there that night when he witnessed him shoot somebody, but when he thinks, he thinks he was wearing a Polo shirt. Mr. Brown says that he saw the shooters out there that night, and he was very firm about it he said Mr. West was wearing a maroon jersey with white letters.

It's probably appropriate now to talk about some of the other identifications, too. Mr. Fields says he saw Mr. West in dark pants and a cap. That's a pretty clear thing to see.

There is nobody else in this case that identifies Mr. West out there that night as wearing a cap. Jerome Sampson says that Kenneth West was wearing a red shirt when he saw him, the red shirt he was wearing in the photo spread. Remember the picture of him in the photo spread with that red shirt, which isn't anything like any of the other descriptions. Mr. Risher says there were three or four people shooting. Mr. Brown says I saw him clearly and there were two people shooting. Mr. Risher has people shooting at distances from each other, one on one side of the car and one on the other side of the car. Mr. Brown says, no, there were two people shooting, one of them was wearing, Kenneth West was wearing a maroon jersey with white letters. Christopher White was wearing a blue jersey with white letters, and they were standing shoulder to shoulder. Now, these are not small differences. These are the kind of differences that make you think they saw two different shootings.

I would admit that people see things differently, but not this differently. This is not proof beyond a reasonable doubt that Kenneth West was the shooter in this case. It can't be. Let's turn to Miss Bluitt's testimony. Remember the lady that we called to the witness stand? The State says that she was not forthcoming with her testimony. In an attempt to compare her with the fact Risher and Brown were not forthcoming, it's extremely important when you assess the testimony of these witnesses, and that you take into consideration what their involvement in the case is. Miss Bluitt was not a witness to the shooting, so in terms of realizing how important her testimony is, there is certainly a difference there. She did not love Sammy Johnson. She didn't even know him. She is by no means close to Kenneth West. And, the fact that she did not run down to the police station, especially in that neighborhood and under those circumstances is understandable. I think her testimony is credible and more important than that, that she doesn't have any reason, known or unknown to us, to lie. And, what she tells us is credible.

Remember Officer Baldwin's testimony that there were probably three shooters out there from the physical evidence? There were probably three shooters out there. She sees running away from the area of the shooting three people, and one of them, probably all of them had them, but she sees one of them with a gun. And, I think that it's--and none of these people are Kenneth West. But, I think it's important, I think it's significant that she says she saw the one with the gun wearing, she says that the one with the gun was wearing a blue jersey with white letters and that he had a gun. This is like the testimony of Mr. Brown. Only Mr. Brown identified Christopher White as the person wearing this blue jersey with white letters. She identifies Cha Cha as having a gun, running away from the shooting and wearing a blue jersey with white letters. Maybe Cha-Cha is the shooter instead of Christopher White. It certainly raises a reasonable doubt in light of Mr. Brown's testimony.

And the other thing is, of course, her testimony is inconsistent with Mr. Risher and Mr. Brown and I think it is incumbent upon you to ask the question, who do you believe beyond a reasonable doubt? Whose testimony would you act upon without hesitation in the most important of your own affairs - Mr. Risher or Mr. Brown or Miss Bluitt's in reconciling those circumstances?

Beyond all this, we have what I think is one of the most significant problems in the prosecution's case." Mr. Irvin turned out to be a better speaker than expected and even though he spoke with the pomp of an Oxford English professor and with about as much enthusiasm as a funeral director, his summation was straight forward. He was telling the jury something's not right about this case, something doesn't add up. Out of fifteen hundred people, the only people who put a gun in the defendant's hand where friends of the victim - two people with the most motivation to lie or to let themselves be influence by an overeager, frustrated detective. The only weakness in his argument was that he wasn't more versed in the scientific aspects of eyewitness testimony or what the latest research was. Had he been, he could've explained to the jury the other factors that perhaps played a part in his client being wrongfully identified as Mr. Johnson's killer.

Nevertheless, it was hard to say how much attention the jury was paying to the various facts Mr. Irvin was painstakingly highlighting or exactly how effective his summation was in jury's mind. But something he said riled the prosecutor up and he was suddenly on his feet.

"I object to his personal opinion about things over and over again."

That objection was the first of many. At this point, the friendly walk-in-the park act had disappeared. This was war. Fire was in his eyes. It wouldn't take long before anyone who made the mistake of underestimating Baldassano to recognize his mistake. The charismatic, unassuming game-show host exterior concealed an iron will. He was here to win by any means necessary and this smooth talking defense attorney with his Ivy League degree and Kentucky Derby manners wasn't about to stop him.

After the Judge overruled his objection, Mr. Irvin continued, "What I feel is extremely significant in this case is the incredibility, the unbelieveability that Kenneth West would shoot into a car of people that he doesn't know, of people who don't know him, of people that he's never had any trouble with before. This is why Mr. Baldassano talked to you about motive in voir dire. And he says to you, you know you can convict a person even though you don't find a motive for the crime. And, that's true. The question for you is do you want to? The State knows it's hard for a jury to do that. It's hard for a jury for there to be absolutely no explanation for a crime. It's hard for a jury to convict without a motive. Now, it makes absolutely no sense whatsoever for Mr. West to do that. So, we roll all of this stuff together, the incredibility of all of the testimony, together with the fact that he doesn't have a motive for doing this and it can't do anything but create in all of your minds a reasonable doubt about whether Mr. West did this.

And, I think that the State realizes this. And, that the State has a problem in this case. But, what does the State do about their problem? They bring another case in here, what they claim is a murder case in here. They try to push you over the edge. The equation goes something like this: One murder case without motive beyond a reasonable doubt, plus another case without motive beyond a reasonable doubt equals one conviction. Don't go for this. Don't let that happen to you. You have to keep the burden of proof in mind at all times. And remember what you have been instructed about the extraneous offense - that's what we call it. It's this other case that came in here in the middle of this case, the one we are concerned with. The court has charged you in relation to that evidence. You cannot consider such evidence for any purpose unless you find and believe beyond a reasonable doubt that the defendant committed such other offense or offenses, if any and there is no proof of beyond a reasonable doubt of this other offense. And I think that the State's own witnesses create such reasonable doubt. Remember the first witness they called? Mr. St. Romain got on the witness stand and testified that he was with Kenneth West over at the parking lot at Carrington's and that Kenneth West expressed a fear that these four guys in the car that was shot up at the Exxon station were going to rob him. But, he didn't have any trouble with them there. He leaves the parking lot, drives off to the Exxon station and this is important, the four people in the car follow him over there.

Once again Baldassano was on his feet, "I object to that as being outside the evidence[17]; it was just the opposite."

[17]Actually it was in the evidence Jacoric Alexander had testified, "I looked at him and at the time he was looking at the car rolling up." T.T Volume 6, pg 60. In street parlance, "rolling up" means the same thing as "driving or pulling up." Perhaps the prosecutor was unaware of the semantics.

The court interjected, "The jury heard the evidence. You will be governed, ladies and gentlemen, by your recollection of what the evidence was.

Mr. Irvin tried to get back started, "And then he testifies to what? This business of seeing the individual in the back seat who ended up being killed, reach for a gun."

The word gun hadn't fully left the defense lawyers mouth before Baldassano was loudly voicing his objection, "I object to that as being outside the evidence."

The Judge sustained Baldassano's objection but Don Irvin was in the groove and kept rolling, "And, hearing Christopher White say, they have a gun. The way the evidence came out, it sounded to me like Christopher White yells "They have a gun." This is St. Romain testifying, still, the State's witness. St. Romain says that Kenneth West pushes him out of the way. Why would Kenneth West push St. Romain out of the way? Out of the way of what? The logical answer is gunfire. They did have a gun, or why would Mr. West push his friend out of the way? And, then Mr. St. Romain runs. If Mr. St. Romain didn't believe that there was a gun in that car, why would he run away? The obvious answer is there was a gun in that car. He gets back into the car and Christopher White says, "I saw the guy's gun." That's what the State's witness testifies to. Also, Jacoric Alexander, who was in the car and had his cousin behind him - his cousin was the person who ended up being shot and killed in the case - admitted he doesn't know whether his cousin pulled a gun or not.

But, there is more from our witnesses. Mr. Alvando Ray says he went over to the Exxon station. He saw four guys in a car that looked like they were up to something. And, that he saw a gun brandished by someone in the car. Cerald Bell says he also heard, doesn't know who from, but he also heard the statement, they've got a gun, the same statement that was testified to before. And, it's not somebody talking about Kenneth West and Christopher White.

There are four other things that we get from the State's witnesses that I think are important. One of them is that Officer Wright testified that the left rear door or window would have had to have been open for a gunshot to have come in the car the way it did. So, we have a window down in a situation where there was testimony from all the witnesses the windows were up. We couldn't push a pistol out the window or anything because the windows were up. We know at least one window was down, or maybe the door was open.

Another thing that's important Officer Wright testified to, and that is, all of the shots that came into the car are concentrated in the area where the dead man was. You can see that from the pictures. What's significant about that is that the shooting is toward this individual, and he's the man who reaches for the gun. He's the man who pulls the gun out, and it helps to explain why the shots came in toward him.

Officer Allen testifies that the bullets and the casings in this case, talking about the Exxon parking lot case as opposed to the Carrington's parking lot case, that these bullet casings and bullets do not match up in terms of coming from the same guns. And, this evidence is supposed to convince you that because Kenneth West was involved in this incident at the Exxon station, that it most probable that he shot at someone in the parking lot at Carrington's.

A very important part of this case Officer Allen testified to is this business of how Kenneth West became a suspect in the Carrington's parking lot shooting. The way it happened was he was a suspect in this other shooting, and in the process of investigating that case, they took pictures of Kenneth West - this is how Kenneth West is lucky enough to get his picture in the photo spread, and have it shown to people. It's a terrifying thought. I wouldn't want my picture in the photo spread and shown to people and say, was he out there; did he shoot? The way that happened was they took that picture from the investigation in the Exxon case, and started showing it to people in this other case. If you look at this, Christopher White and Kenneth West are the only ones that really look alike in that photo spread. See how this works? That's why Kenneth West ends up in this case.

This isn't proof beyond a reasonable doubt in either one of these alleged offenses. And, the reason this isn't proof beyond a reasonable doubt in either one of these alleged offenses is that Kenneth West in the Exxon case was defending himself and in the other case he was not a shooter. Kenneth West is not guilty of the crime he's charged with here.

Now, there are a lot of things that go unsaid in jury argument. You forget things. You only have a certain amount of time to talk. But, there is one thing in particular that I want to say to you and that is that you all must make up your mind about whether or not there is a reasonable doubt in this case. But, if you have a reasonable doubt after considering all of the evidence about whether or not Kenneth West shot at the car that Sammie Johnson was in that night, if you have a reasonable doubt, grapple it to your hearts with bands of steel, because it's important, and don't let anybody bully you out of that doubt. Thank you very much."

When Mr. Irvin took his seat the juror's eyes rested on the defendant, a chubby baby-faced young man the juror's eyes seemed to be asking the same question, "Did you do this thing? Are you a cold blooded killer?"

At that moment, it was possible a few jurors still harbored a "reasonable doubt," however the prosecutor didn't. In his mind Kenneth West was the devil and it was his task, his solemn duty to convince these twelve honest men and women to excise this devil right up out of society; hopefully forever.

Standing erect, Baldassano shook his head, then flashed his trademark smile, "Well, you have to Delliberate. You can't go back there and just not talk. I enjoyed the defense attorney's argument. I think it's a good argument. The first ten minutes and the part about George Washington and all, I really liked that. I am nodding my head and thinking that sounds like - I started thinking, that's his generic argument. That's the argument you use in every case. But, going through the witnesses, let me talk about some of the things he mentioned. Look for yourself at the photos. There is a video tape. The lights are there in the photographs, right around the tire store and the liquor store. And, it's lit by rows and rows of lights in the parking lot. And, maybe it's not as bright as the sun, but it's pretty bright out there. You can see that by looking at the lights in the photograph, independent of the type of film used. The lights are in the photographs. Also, not in the photographs, are the headlights of the cars were on. We know they are all over the parking lot, some with their headlights on.

Let me talk about the witnesses and their motive. I think the defense really did throw up their arms and say, I don't know. Why did the guys come and lie? That's what they would have to be doing. Maybe Lawrence Fields, if we put on a case and it was just Lawrence Fields, maybe you feel that would be tough to believe beyond a reasonable doubt; maybe not. The other guys and he did pick him out of a line-up. The other guys are positive. Are they lying or not? Why would they lie? The defense counsel doesn't come up with any reasonable answer why they would.

First of all, if they love Sammie Johnson, you would think they have a motive to get the guy who killed him, the right guy. Why him? There is absolutely no evidence they would want to get him in prison or get him in trouble? What kind of story is it for a young kid to be making up a case against a guy like Kenneth West who has a bunch of friends and where the guys all go to the same clubs? You might not want to be a witness. You might be reluctant to be a witness generally. Certainly you wouldn't want to go in the clubs and say to this guy's friends you made up this case against him. I suggest to you that's an easy way to get yourself killed. Maybe people said Kenneth West got what he deserved; maybe not what he deserved. Maybe nobody will bother them for that. Certainly these guys don't want to be involved. They certainly don't have any motive, certainly no reason to tell you that. They did tell you what they saw, and didn't see, and kind of let the chips fall where they may. We know they were close. Risher and Brown said there were no obstructions. You could see that from the photographs. There are no trees or poles or anything out there. They were right there. Their statements match the physical evidence. You can see from the diagram from where they were parked is where all of these shells ended up. The shells ended up right here, where the lights are. There is light all over, and shells all over. You know from Robert Baldwin's testimony, you know the guns spit out a round maybe five feet. They are round. They rolled as a result. All of them roll in the same direction. We know it's pretty flat out there from the testimony. So, we know the guys doing the shooting are right next to them. We know that matches. We see from the condition of the car their testimony is pretty accurate. This is the victim's car where Sammie Johnson was in. And, we know every time they are shown a picture of the defendant, they positively identify him. They never misidentify him. You can see the photo spread in evidence. You can open the photo spread and look at the other photo spread, and there are signatures right across the front. They are absolutely positive; never misidentified him. They recognized him. They know him.

Lawrence Fields. I think the significant thing about Lawrence Fields is he doesn't know Kenneth West or Christopher White. He picks them both out. How could he know that? We know they hang out together. It's just a great coincidence in the photo spread of five young black males he picks those two and only those two? I think it's significant to you he picks them out because he saw them there. He has nothing to gain. Certainly they love Sammie Johnson. Certainly they want to see the right guy get convicted.

Jessie Brown, again, he never makes any misidentification. I'm not going to harp on that.

Larry Risher, I think, is most significant. He knows the defendant, not by name. He said that. But, he knows him because he has seen him in the club before. He's seen him around. That's reasonable. They are at the same club that night. These young guys go to the same clubs. He's seen him before. He doesn't want to get involved in a shooting that happened with a bunch of people, and you saw it, and you run and you didn't talk to the police that night. You thought that the person that did it was arrested. Maybe you wouldn't have to come forward. There is no reason to come forward. No motive to come forward to be testifying against some other guy in the neighborhood. Maybe you don't want to do that. Maybe you should, but you don't. But, you know there were officers doing extra jobs out there. I suggest to you they take off just as fast. That's the way people are. If you don't think the follow-up investigation is important, maybe we should tell Sergeant Allen and Abby, don't do it. Later, nobody is going to believe you. Fine. Follow-up is most important because people take off when a crime happens. That's the way it is. The reason the guys who testified knew the complainant is the guys in the car could only give to the police names of people that they knew out there to talk to.

And, we know some of these guys saw it. So, go talk to these guys, and that's what they did. And, then when he talks to them, they take a written statement, and it's about a month later. Certainly not a year and a half later, like Bluitt and Alvando Ray, or whatever his name was. I suggest to you that maybe it's not the greatest way to be for society in general for people to run from a crime scene, but that's the way it is. That does happen.

I want to call your attention to Bluitt. That girl, I don't know. I think she does stand for the proposition though that people leave. The one thing that is interesting, though, is the difference between Brown and Risher. They think the guy that did the shooting was arrested, so they don't do anything. But, hers is just the opposite. She thinks her friend is arrested for something he didn't do. That's a little different than thinking the guys who did it got arrested, and lay back and don't do anything. That's one thing. He's some relation to the family. I think on cross examination--maybe not-- something about the baby's husband's cousin or something like that, but she knows Kenneth West is wrongfully arrested. She doesn't do anything, doesn't say anything, not a word, nothing. And, she saw Cha-Cha with a gun. If all of the evidence we brought on the murder case against Cha-Cha was he was running by Arby's, I think you would find him not guilty in five seconds.

MR. ERVIN: Objection; arguing outside the record.

THE COURT: Stay within the record.

MR. BALDASSANO: Maybe Kenneth West split off and goes the other way when he sees someone he knows. Maybe she doesn't see him; maybe a lot of things. She certainly doesn't see the shooting, and it's certainly not all that important. She certainly doesn't tell the police about anything at all, or anybody, for a year and a half.

One thing I think is significant. I mentioned the defendant doesn't have to testify. That's clear. I'm not commenting on that. But, they don't contest he's out there in the crowded parking lot. They have said that several times. Well, if he's out there by their own admission in the crowded parking lot, and they want to bring you a witness, why not bring you people in the crowd he was with? Hey, there was a shooting. He was standing next to me in the crowd. That would be important evidence; not the Bluitt girl who's at the Arby's.

Let me talk about the extraneous. I think it's important. On the extraneous case, again, you don't even have to believe it happened. We didn't have to present that case to you to find this defendant guilty of killing Sammie Johnson. That's the case we have. But, certainly in the extraneous the identity of the defendant is not contested. I think even in his final argument, the defense attorney said he might have done it, and his defense is self defense in this case, but he did it. I think that's important to show the identity that Lawrence Fields and Larry Risher and Jessie Brown aren't slapping themselves in the chest like three crazy people that made up some pie in the sky thing they felt one day, that they said the name of Kenneth West and they had to go and convict him. I think that shows some identity. I am going to show you on the board here--I don't know if you can read it. First of all, they want you to believe that that's self-defense. This car was attacked like this in self-defense. This car looks like it was parked on the dock during the attack of Pearl Harbor. This is not self-defense. There are two types of shells out there.

We heard the officer testify there are two shooters. We know that that's really not contested. That is not contesting there were two types of shells out there only. This car was wracked with bullets and bullet fragments and bullet casing out there. There were two guns, him and Christopher White. That's it. For those other guys parked there first, while one of them was going to the bathroom, while packed in there, to start waving a gun around would probably be suicide. It doesn't make any sense anybody would do that. Even if they did, this isn't self-defense. You can't shoot people in the back and claim self-defense[18]; that's not self-defense. Just by the grace of God - I always hated those cars with the big speakers, but now I'm thinking of getting one. That saved a lot of lives, those big speakers. They are so noisy, but they probably saved a couple of lives. That's not self-defense even if he came out with an anti-aircraft gun, because you have got to run away.

Now it was the Oxford's man turn to object and the erudite Mr. Irvin slowly rose to his feet, "I object to him arguing law that is not before the jury."

What the prosecutor was attempting to do was highlight an arcane principle in Texas's self-defense law known as the "duty to retreat." What this 1973 addition to the self-defense law basically said was that before someone could claim self-defense under existing Texas law they had to first show they tried to retreat from the conflict.

---

[18]Under 9.31 of the Texas Penal Code, section b, a person is justified in using force against another when and to the degree he reasonably believes the force is immediately necessary to protect himself against the other's use or attempted use of unlawful force. There is nowhere in the Penal Code that uses an individual's injury to determine if self-defense occurred.

In 2008, the Texas legislature recognized this provision was a mistake that attempting to retreat in most situations that called for the use of "deadly" force was essentially a death sentence. As a result, House Bill 284 along with Senate Bill 378 collectively known as the Castle Doctrine abolished this provision. Another amazing aspect of the prosecutor's argument against the defendant's self-defense claim was that at the same time Harris County was seeking to put Kenneth West in prison, police officers and city officials were busy arguing the exact opposite in the Pedro Oregon case.

Acting on information from a bad informant that Pedro Oregon was dealing drugs, Houston Police Officers burst into Mr. Oregon's apartment. In fear, Mr. Oregon ran to his bedroom and the officers thinking he had a gun began shooting. In all, five police officers fired a total of 33 rounds. Out of the 12 bullets that struck Mr. Oregon, nine hit him in the back. Even more incredible was the fact that one of the police officers, David R. Barrera, fired 24 of the 33 rounds. By first unloading his entire 16-round magazine, then reloading and firing 8 more rounds, the whole time Pedro Oregon was faced down on his bedroom floor. Nevertheless, a grand jury found that the officers acted in self-defense.

Commenting on the case and the nobilled officers to the Houston Chronicle on November 5, 1998 Harris County District Attorney John B. Holmes who at the time was Baldassano's boss said "State law allows police officers to use deadly force if they believe it necessary for self-defense and they can continue shooting so long as they reasonably perceive the threat continues."

He went on to say, "An analogy I use is that if it is ok to kill a guy dead, it is ok to kill him dead, dead, dead." Magazine emptied and reloaded - self-defense; unarmed, shot nine times in the back – self-defense.

So while his boss was saying one thing to the Houston Chronicle, Baldassano was in front of the jurors in the 176th district courtroom telling them something completely different. Obviously, the District Attorney's office had another policy when it came to average citizens like the defendant.

Baldassano continued, "Take a look at the fact on State's Exhibit 117, all the shells are in one spot. They may have sprayed the car over like that, but the shells and the one that goes through the open window, if it's open is certainly not on the side with the guy with the gun, or the guy I don't know what he's doing. They are certainly not on the run. They are concentrated. You don't have people running for their own protection. They are not running; they are shooting. That's not self-defense. Look at the board. Look how similar those cases are. That does show identity, this person's identity. He's the same person who did the shooting of Sammie Ray Johnson, Jr. I think the most significant thing is he does it with the same guy, Christopher White.

I think the evidence is clear in this case. One other thing, this was brought up by the defense otherwise I wouldn't mention it. The defense attorney asked Sergeant Waymon Allen "Did he tell you it was self-defense?" "No." "What did he tell you?" "I don't know anything about it."

On this point Baldassano was clearly misrepresenting the facts. Sgt. Allen had testified that the defendant chose to exercise his constitutional right to counsel.

Q: By the way, when you talked to Kenneth and you asked him for a statement, did he request to be allowed to have an attorney present before he gave a written statement.

A: Well, the answer to that would be yes.

Q: Was one provided for him?

A: No, the interview was terminated.

Q: So, he just asked to have an attorney? It wasn't like he wasn't going to give you a statement? He just wanted an attorney there when he gave it, is this correct?

A: Well, he invoked his rights.

A prosecutor who didn't vigorously pursue what he believed to be his version of the facts wouldn't be living up to his obligations. Nevertheless, the concept of justice signifies certain lines not be crossed. Dishonesty, in any form, crosses that ethical line.

But it seemed in the prosecutor's book, it was too late in the game to be concerned with such small things as ethics and he continued to press two erroneous points related to the extraneous offense. That the amount of force could somehow be used as a determinant of if a case was self-defense or not, and that since the defendant didn't walk up to the police and give a statement without the present of his attorney then therefore it wasn't.

The prosecutor continued, "That seems like a stretch. You would think you would remember something like that. You pump a ton of bullets into a car you would think you'd remember, instead of saying, yeah, man, it was self-defense. Let me explain all of those bullet holes because these guys pulled a weapon on me. Let me explain. I don't know anything about it. You know all about it. You know these two cars get shot up. It looks like Custer's last stand with these poles in the car and this Sammie

Ray Johnson. And we know the defendant walked around the front of both cars right before the shooting.

I don't pretend to know why anybody would shoot anybody like this. I don't think there is ever a good reason. It looks like they started getting in the eye thing, with the eyes. I guess in the green car at the Exxon. I suggest to you that's the same thing that happened. No good reason. No motive for doing anything like that. That's probably what it was about looking tough and acting tough and doing something stupid and that's what they did. I suggest to you the evidence is overwhelming this defendant is guilty beyond a reasonable doubt of killing this man who had no reason to die that night on June 6, 1997. He's guilty beyond a reasonable doubt and probably beyond all doubt based on what you have heard and I think you should find him guilty. Thank you." Baldassano sat down.

At that point the judge turned the case over to the jury, "Thank you ladies and gentlemen. If you would please retire to the jury room and begin your Delliberations. Let us know just as quickly as you have arrived at a verdict."

The jury left the room and the defendant hung his head. They were going to convict him, he could feel it. Not because the evidence of his guilt was so overwhelming like the prosecutor said, it wasn't. In fact, it was nothing of the sort. He was being railroaded and they knew it. In his mind once the judge allowed the extraneous offense to be admitted he no longer had a chance. That was the moment he lost the trial; from then on, it was just a matter of going through the process; the outcome was inevitable.

So with the jury out, they waited. The general rule of Delliberations was for the defense the longer the better. Most acquittals resulted from long Delliberations. Short Delliberations normally indicated a guilty verdict.

They began Delliberations at 9:45 a.m. and at 10:02, a request came from the jury room, "May we have the photos and photo spread and diagrams of the parking lot at Carrington's and Exxon."

The defense attorneys were encouraged by this development. For the defendant just the fact that they requested anything was a good sign. Contrary to the joke the prosecutor made about them having to Delliberate, their request seemed to show that they were really engaged in the sacred honor Don Irvin alluded to in his opening statement.

Thirty minutes later, more encouraging news came from the jury room, "May we please have the written witness statements to police."

The judge replied to the juror's request, "As related to the court's charge, you may consider any of the evidence admitted before you - the items you requested are not in the evidence."

The defendant allowed himself to hope ever so slightly. Would this jury be able to see past the prosecutor's dirty tricks? And simply try him on the merits and evidence of the case he was currently on trial for? Or, would they lump the two into one as the prosecutor was hoping?

Another hour; sixty more spine-tingling, panic-inducing minutes crawled by at a snail's pace.

At 11:39 the wait was over; the jury signaled they had a verdict. They had been Delliberating for an hour and fifty-four minutes. The jury filed into the room and took their seats. The defendant tried to make eye contact, but no one returned his gesture.

The judge addressed the foreman, "Mr. Foreman, has your jury arrived at a verdict?"

"Yes, we have. We, the jury, find the defendant, Kenneth West, guilty of murder as charged in the indictment."

Chapter Six - No Defense

Elated by the quick victory Baldassano was fired up and ready to go. The defendant's trial for the death of Efrem Breaux was scheduled to begin the same week.

By now the defendant was numb. He came to court every day but wasn't there. He didn't understand how he could get convicted for a murder he didn't commit. Was that justice? And if they could make him guilty of a shooting he didn't have anything to do with, what chance did he have in this case? Even if it was self-defense? What did it matter? Without some type of concrete evidence that the prosecutor couldn't manipulate or twist it didn't matter. He was at his lowest and didn't think things could get any worse. But even the bottom had a basement. During the previous trial Don Irvin had told the judge that if he allowed the jury to hear evidence of the other murder in the guilt or innocence phase the trial would no longer be a contest. Inherit in his argument was the belief that such proceedings were ever meant to be a, "fair contest." Now as the defense geared up for a second trial in the same courtroom Baldassano sought to put a end to such naive assumptions by going from, "No Contest," to "No Defense."

Before having this bombshell dropped in his lap, the defendant planned to pursue a straight forward self-defense claim in the death of Efrem Breaux. Yes he had shot Mr. Breaux but only after he pulled a gun on him and his two friends Christopher White and Chirstopher St. Romain.

For proof he planned to take the stand and explain to the jury what happened and why. Before the first trial he had felt confident he would win an acquittal. His testimony was supported by the state's main witness, along with three defense witnesses:

Alvando Ray, Cerald Bell and Edward Josey (Pop). Each witness supported his self-defense claim.

And Edward Josey recollection was better than expected. He was prepared to testify that his Chevy Tahoe was behind Jacoric's green Hyundai when it was struck in the front grill by a single bullet and that he saw the driver jump out with something small in his hand that he believed was a gun.

The only difference in the state's case from their presentation in the extraneous was the addition of a HPD firearm expert, a coroner and two additional witnesses Jacobe Smith and D'Eric Carney - the other two passengers in the car. Their testimony was that they didn't have any guns or knives in their car, nor did they have any type of conflict with anyone. Essentially they were out minding their business after a night on the town when they noticed the defendant looking strange; after that, somebody shot up their car and killed their friend for no reason. In a nutshell, that was the state's case.

In a world where justice and truth meant more than convictions, the new jury seated in Honorable Bob Burdette's courtroom would hear all the evidence relevant to the death of Efrem Breaux from both the prosecutor and the defense. And their subsequent verdict would be based on the evidence they heard from both sides since truth was always simple and justice and truth were synonymous. That was the way most people believed it worked.

Unfortunately for the defendant, he was being tried in Harris County and justice in Harris County under Johnny B.Holmes and his predecessor

Chuck Rosenthial was whatever the prosecutors said it was. If they decided you were guilty, then you were guilty. All the evidence or witnesses in the world wouldn't change it.

The defendant knew what this meant; he had just received a stiff dose of this medicine and didn't expect this trial to be much different.

Baldassano didn't disappoint him; he waited until the state finished presenting all of its evidence before playing his trump card. Once the state rested, as the defense was about to begin calling their witnesses, the shoe dropped.

E.J. Van Buren and Baldassano had a sidebar outside the presence of the jury. When Van Buren returned to the defense table, he told his client that the prosecutor had just informed him that if they put on any type of defense case, or if he took the stand, then he was going to seek to have evidence of the extraneous murder that he had just been convicted of admitted into the trial. And since the judge allowed it to be admitted in the guilt or innocence phase of the last trial, there was no question about whether or not he would allow it. He had already proved his fidelity to hang 'em high style justice.

The defendant was dumbstruck if the extraneous was admitted into this trial the way it was in the last one, there was no question in his mind of if he would be convicted. The last jury convicted him in under two hours without one iota of evidence.

He looked at Van Buren, "They can't do this; how can this be a trial if I can't testify or put on witnesses?"

Van Buren let the question hang in the air knowing that there was really no answer he could give him.

With Baldassano looking and waiting for their decision, Van Buren reiterated what he had just told him - the only way they could keep the extraneous out was if he didn't testify, or put on any defense witnesses. That meant the jury would never hear from Alvando Ray, Cerald Bell or Edward Josey. No defense case would be allowed.

Baldassano was offering no other options - challenge the state case and face the extraneous. Now the genesis of his entire trial strategy was fully revealed.

He had pushed hard to go to trial on the weaker case first knowing that if he won that one, using the two cases in one strategy, he could later use the conviction to prevent the defendant from mounting an effective self-defense claim.

Whether such a strategy was ethical or served the purpose of justice was questionable, however it was effective. It left no margin of error for the prosecutor. No witnesses = no defense.

Van Buren tried to explain to the defendant that his only chance of winning an acquittal was to use the state's witnesses to raise the self-defense issue without actually putting on any defense witnesses or testifying.

But the defendant was livid, "Ya'll railroading me," he said. "Why the hell you let me come to trial? You shoulda been explained this shit. I can't win and you know it."

He was upset that Van Buren waited until the trial was already underway and they were at a crisis moment to tell him for the first time that he couldn't testify or present any witnesses without facing sanctions. With a set-up like that, he never had a chance. And Van Buren had accepted his mother's hard earned money while selling her son out the entire time.

By not advising and preparing him for the strategy the state was most likely to pursue, being that he was facing two cases, Don Irvin and E.J Van Buren had done him a profound disservice and robbed him of the opportunity to make an informed decision.

In his first trial, he never heard the word "extraneous offense," until he heard Baldassano arguing to have it admitted in the trial. Now, Van Buren had done the same thing - waited until it was too late to try to inform him of what was going on.

Van Buren knew he had screwed up; you don't lead a client on for months with a trial strategy that included him testifying and putting on witnesses to prove his case then once the trial starts, turn around and say, "I made a mistake we can't do it like that."

Therefore once again Van Buren began trying to cover up his professional misconduct and ineffective assistance of counsel in anticipation of the State Bar grievances and ineffective counsel claims to come.

Essentially his was the "I was just following orders defense." But what defendant in his right mind would go to trial knowing they weren't going to be allowed to prove their innocence; that defeated the purpose. That's why the defendant consistently maintained his innocence telling anyone who would listen that he didn't get a fair trial and that Harris County railroaded him. And that had his attorney's adequately prepared him, he doubted that he would've went to trial. How could anyone prove their innocence if the prosecutor who was supposed to be an agent of justice flat out said if you put on a defense, any defense, regardless of how truthful it may be, I'll use strategy that will get you convicted anyway.

But the defendant wasn't taking this laying down. There was turmoil at the defense table when Van Buren stood up in the nearly empty courtroom. By now, client and attorney were barely speaking. The defendant was trying to determine exactly who he hated the most – Baldassano for his underhanded tactics or Van Buren for selling him out, or himself for being naive enough to believe he would receive a fair trial or that trials had anything to do with truth and justice.

Even though the proceedings were about him, at this point, he only half listened to the judge. They had made it clear, his input didn't matter. By now he was a passenger on the train of his own destiny. Harris County was taking him where they wanted him to go, and Van Buren had helped him get on the train; the conviction train.

The Court: Mr. Van Buren, as we all know here in the courtroom, let the record reflect, before the noon recess, the state rested their evidence in the case. That was about 11:30 a.m. and it is now 1:16 p.m., that being an hour and forty-six minutes later. And before the jury is brought in, is there anything you care to get on record?

The defendant stared at the judge for the last hour he had been arguing with his attorney and had accused him of selling him out. Now he believed the judge was in on it too, he knew what was going on, had seen the drama at the defense table now here he was asking Van Buren was there anything he wanted to get on record. It was a scratch my back I'll scratch your back type of deal and the only one getting screwed was the defendant.

Van Buren: Yes, your Honor. And this is in regards to my representation of Kenneth West in this matter. Mr. West, you understand the position we're at right now. The state having rested in the case and not moved to reopen the evidence in any fashion, correct?

West: Yeah

Van Buren: And you and I have discussed at great length the possible trial strategies from this point on, correct?

West: Yeah

Van Buren: Now you understand, at this point, the self-defense issue has been raised and evidence regarding that issue has been discussed by and through various witnesses, most particular in association with the testimony of Christopher St. Romain, correct?

West: Yeah

Van Buren: Now the question is: At this point, do we put on any witnesses. And first off, I have shown you a copy of the testimony of Jacoric Alexander from Cause No.771595 which was the previous trial of an allegation of murder against you that I participated in but was not the lead attorney on correct? I showed you this and I informed you that I'd ordered this last night and you saw me pay for it this morning when she brought it, right?

West: Yeah

Van Buren: And that was documentation that I could utilize to impeach the witness with prior inconsistent statements, correct?

West: Yes

Van Buren: That would require him coming back to the witness stand, which would mean we would be putting on a defense case. Additionally we have three witnesses present on your behalf whose names, of course you refer to them by their nicknames but their true and correct names are Cerald Bell and Alvando Ray, correct? And you know that they were properly subpoenaed and in fact they have been present outside the courtroom for at least the past two days, right?

West: Yeah

Van Buren: The third one, where just final arrangement were completed whereby a subpoena was served for Edward Josey who was found to be in a state jail facility, Joe Kegans Jail facility and you know that that individual is present back in the holdover cell right now, right?

West: Yeah

The judge interrupted, "Excuse me, I apologize for interrupting. If I'm understanding correctly, each of these three people who you have subpoenaed and caused to be present here in the court today, at the outset through Mr. West, you were only given a street name or nick-name?"

Van Buren: That's correct.

The judge went on, "Only as a result of your investigation, you found out who those people were, in fact and were able to get them in court?" At this point, it was plain the judge was no longer acting as an unbiased observer. Having sat through the trial, he knew first hand that E.J Van Buren's representation of his client fell well below the minimum standards required by the law. And knowing they were on the record, he was trying to combat an ineffective assistance of counsel claim along with a possible reversal by advocating for the quality of the defense attorney's representation. It was so blatant, that even Van Buren recognized what the judge was doing.

Van Buren: That's correct. Thank you, Judge. All three witnesses are available to present evidence that would potentially be helpful to your defense in this case, correct?

West: Yes

Van Buren: And finally, there have been discussions as to whether or not you yourself would testify in this case, correct?

West: Yeah

Van Buren: And we discussed your desire to be heard in that regard as well as some of the complications that would be in effect should you take the witness stand, correct?

West: Yes

Van Buren: Now, you and I discussed the fact that at this point, that if we put on even one witness and in anyway present a defense case, it will open the door, present the opportunity for the state to present rebuttal testimony, which in this circumstance, would be the extraneous offense of murder that was previously tried in this very courtroom, correct?

West: Yes

Van Buren: And I discussed my feelings about the effect that I felt that would have on the jury compared to the possible probative value of the witnesses that were present, correct?

West: Yes

Van Buren: You and I discussed this at great length correct?

West: Yes

Van Buren: Ultimately, is it your decision to have any witnesses presented as part of your defense in this case or is it your decision to rest at this time and allow us to just proceed on the information that is before the jury; that is evidence that is before the jury at the present time?

Van Buren had led his client between a rock and a hard place and the defendant didn't know what to do. A few months earlier, he had converted to Christianity and he desperately wanted to take the stand in his own defense. Just to have the chance to tell what happened and he wanted his witnesses to testify. But, after the hour and fifty-six minute outcome of his last trial with the extraneous hanging over his head, doing so would be equivalent to suicide.

He was stuck and the one word answers he gave his attorney seemed about as voluntary as an American P.O.W with a machine gun to his head renouncing his U.S citizenship.

Van Buren: And you're doing that freely voluntarily right?

West: (Hesitantly) Yeah

Van Buren: And you're satisfied that I'm doing my very, very best for you as it applies to your representation in this case?

West: Yeah, I guess.

With that, the defense rested, without calling one witness. Predictably with nothing to rely on except the State's version of what transpired at the Exxon station on November 9, 1996 the jury found the defendant guilty of killing 23 year old Efrem Breaux.

Once the verdict was read, the defendant turned and mouthed, "Don't cry," to his mother. He needed her to be strong; if she broke, he wouldn't be far behind.

Chapter Seven - Unrehabilitable

Prior to being convicted, the defendant took his attorney's advice and opted to be sentenced by the judge as opposed to the jury should he be found guilty. Now that dreaded moment had arrived and after a brief presentencing investigation, the defendant and his attorneys reassembled in the 176th District Court.

There were two matters on the court's agenda; the most obvious was the sentence the judge would pronounce. But of equal importance, because Baldassano had filed a motion to stack the sentences, was if the judge would grant the motion. If he did, it meant whatever sentences the defendant received, he would have to complete one before beginning the other. Generally, such harsh sentences were reserved for the worst of worst repeat offenders who had cycled in and out the system on multiple occasions; nevertheless, Baldassano felt the defendant warranted such a sentence.

Worst had came to worse for the defendant, the only hope he had of ever seeing the world outside a prison cell rested on his attorney's belief that even though two juries had found him guilty, it was possible the judge still harbored some doubts about the veracity of the evidence against him and if so, he was likely to take it into consideration when pronouncing the sentence and in deciding whether to stack the sentences or not. And, being that the defendant's punishment was to be decided by the judge as opposed to the jury, there were no victim impact statements; all communication relating to the sentencing had been submitted to the judge in written form along with a sentencing memorandum from the defense.

In a ploy to lift the spirits of the defendant and his family, both attorneys feigned cautious optimism. But the defendant saw through it, he expected the worst. The things that had transpired in this courtroom left him with no faith in the court or any of its officers. In his mind, he had experienced a modern day lynching and received as much justice as Emitt Till.

Following the order of the trials, Don Irvin rose and approached the bench and made a last ditch effort to preserve some type of future for his client and ended up giving his most passionate speech of the trial.

He told the judge, "I believe all the evidence that the court has before it, would indicate that Mr. West is a good person in heart who loves his family and his family loves him. He has favorably impressed over the years those persons charged with schooling him and coming into contact with him on a social bases.

I think that that background and that indication of what kind of person that he was as he was growing up is something that the court should take into consideration in sentencing him.

The problem that we have here and what I tried to address in my memorandum is the situation where he embraced at an early age an insane lifestyle involving drugs and violence, and that he had a terrible drug problem that is contemporaneous with these offenses committed in this case, there's reference to that in the pre-sentencing investigation.

And I would that the court would consider, not in defense of course, but in mitigation of his punishment the fact that he had a terrible drug[19] problem and that he embraced this life-style. I believe from talking to him and from talking to his relatives, from all of the information that I have and that the court has before it, that he is someone that has already began the process of rehabilitation, that the good parentage that he had, the good background that he had is something that has came back to the forefront. That he's someone that's very intelligent and who with the will to rehabilitate and the ability to rehabilitate can become a productive citizen whenever he gets out of prison; that he's someone who should be given an opportunity to rehabilitate and to save his life in this society and I hope the court would consider all these things in assessing his punishment," with that, the Dapper Don took his seat.

Since it was incumbent upon Van Buren to make a statement, he stood to say his piece. Throughout the trial, the personal problems that would later lead to him being disbarred were already evident.

As he would show up unkempt and late for court most of the time, he appeared to be functioning purely on instinct and habit; several times the judge had to chasten him for tardiness.

Now, he was prepared to make a plea for the defendant's life, he said, "Specifically as it applies to my representation of Mr. West for the charges alleged and the defense that was asserted, as this Court perhaps was aware that the case was left before in the jury argument in the best possible posture to bring forth the elements by which that defense was worthy of consideration. I don't think any retribution in terms of counting the number of years is going to change the tragedy that's impacted

[19]In hindsight, it seemed that this particular argument should have resonated with judge Burdette. A few years after the West trial, the judge was leaving a local watering hole when he rammed his Jaguar into the back of Lyn Simon's pickup truck. Then in a drunken stupor, he attempted to drive away and had to be physically restrained by several bystanders to keep him from leaving. During the altercation, he told one of them, "I'm drunk, I've got to go home now." The judge made it home after he got out of jail for DWI, however in 2009 he was in trouble with the law again this time for driving with a permanently revoked license.

these individuals, the family, the family in the cause number that I handled.

I would ask in the alternative that the Court consider the factors that had established a defense issue that was submitted to the jury and additionally bear in mind the comments that Mr. Irvin has ably brought forth to the court but also, if I may, just my personal injections that in dealing over the course of these past months with Kenneth West, I have found an individual who does bare scars from the foolish and tragic actions that he took, but at the same time has taken steps to improve himself and is getting involved in things, going during his period of incarceration that may at some point allow him to re-enter society as a person worthy of consideration. I ask this Court not to write off Kenneth West as a human being because that's not going to bring back either of these other human beings. Of course the Court is aware of that. And just bear in mind that I found him to be an individual who I believe is on the road to potential recovery not only with any drug problems but also with the struggle to become a man."

When Van Buren finished rambling, the defendant looked at him the way one would an embarrassing family member who had just acted out in front of company. What was Van Buren talking about? He jumped around so much without elaborating on any one theme that it was likely his statement hurted as much as it helped.

Once the defense lawyers finished saying their piece, it was the prosecutor's turn and Baldassano had a different take.

.He told the judge, "He deserves as much time as you can give him. I suggest two life sentences to run consecutively."

However brief it was it appeared to be more in line with the judge's thinking. Whatever happened, or didn't happen in the trials was irrelevant to him. What was important was that the defendant Kenneth West was unredeemable and unrehabilitatable, completely unfit to be a part of society ever again. The judge wanted his sentence to reflect this, in a booming voice he said, "Stand up, Mr. West."

The defendant stood. Two rows behind him his mother prayed.

"In cause no. 771595, I now assess your punishment at confinement in the institutional division of the Texas Department of Criminal Justice for a period of 60 years."

There was a slight gasp in the courtroom and the judge waited.

Then he continued, "In cause no.768322, I assess your punishment at confinement in the institutional division of the Texas Department of Criminal Justice for a period of 60 years."

With the sentences pronounced there was one matter still before the court, whether to stack the sentences or allow them to run concurrently. For the defendant, this decision was the difference between 30 or 60 years in prison.

In announcing his decision of whether to stack the sentences the judge said, "I am persuaded from that philosophical concept in the sense that to not cumulate (stack) these sentences would in essence give Mr. West a free murder and I am not willing to do that." With that, he proceeded to stack the sentences.

The defendant was a first time offender who had never served TYC time, county jail time, or stepped foot inside of a prison. However, none of that matter in the eyes of the judge and prosecutor; he was unrehabilitatable and the judge had given him a one way ticket to prison. Under the laws in effect at the time of his sentencing, he would be eligible for parole for the first time in 2058 when he was 78 years old.

Chapter Eight - One Hundred Percent Certain

Young and beautiful, Jennifer Thompson was a college student with her whole life in front of her. Then came the fateful night in August of 1984 when her world was shattered.

Raped in her own home she marshaled every inch of resolve she had to keep from passing out while she carefully studied every detail of her attacker's face. A face she would never forget.

The crime rocked the community and within weeks the police had zeroed in on a suspect. All they needed from Mrs. Thompson was for her to come down to the police station and confirm what they already knew. At the station she positively identified 22 year old Ronald Cotton as the man who had brutally raped her first from a photo-lineup, then once again from a live lineup. She was certain, had never been more certain of anything in her life, Ronald Cotton was the man who raped, her.

A year later the case made it to trial. On the witness stand Mrs. Thompson was forced to relive the horrible ordeal all over again. She felt the fear and humiliation anew as if it had happened yesterday.

But it was worth it to keep a monster off the street and to prevent what happened to her from happening to anyone else. The case was an open and shut case based on the concrete identification of the victim. For the jury, the decision was simple, the man had raped her, his face was less than a feet away; it was a no-brainer. But for the sake of the record, the DA took her through the usual, "Do you see the man who raped you in the courtroom today?"

She did and, for the third time, she positively identified Ronald Cotton the man in the defendant's chair.

Once the jury got the case, they didn't waste time doing what they had to do. They found the defendant guilty and sentenced him to life, sending him away to be all but forgotten by society.

Eleven years later, another prisoner, a convicted rapist, bragged about rapping Mrs. Thompson. With the man's confession, the wheels of injustice begin to turn ever so slowly until eventually it was discovered, using DNA testing unavailable at the time of the rape, that it was indeed Bobby Poole who had raped Mrs. Thompson and not Ronald Cotton the man who was serving time for the crime; a crime he didn't commit.

However, when the detectives brought Mr. Poole before Mrs. Thompson, she told them she had never seen him before in her life. Later, when she recounted her ordeal to the New York Times she said, "I was certain, but I was wrong."

That Mrs. Thompson was wrong in her identification of Ronald Cotton as the man who raped her might surprise most people, but not the psychologist who study, "Eyewitness testimony."Contrary to what many people believe the human mind doesn't work like a video camera recording then retrieving information on command, exactly as it was viewed.

Instead, we gather bits and pieces of information, integrate it with what we already know and with additional information we pick up along the way. In that respect human memory is more like a collage then a single portrait. And before information can be adequately or accurately recalled, a three step process has to occur that consist of Acquisition, Retention and Retrieval. Various problems occur at either of these stages that can lead to mistaken identifications.

In addition to the three stage memory process, researchers in the field have discovered several factors related to eyewitness identifications that continue to be problematic and contributing factors to mistaken identifications.

Many of these factors were present in the West case; therefore, they will be examined individually as well as the part they likely played in the defendant's wrongful conviction.

Nevertheless, within the criminal justice community the problem of mistaken identifications is an open secret. A secret that has been consistently swept under the rug until the rug begin to pucker with the number of innocent men exonerated by DNA continuing to climb.

After spending decades arguing that only guilty people were sent to prison and that the system is fair and just, elements within the criminal justice system reluctantly begin to acknowledge the obvious - mistakes are made; innocent people have been sent to prison and possibly executed and the problem still exist.

Acknowledging these facts, Dallas Assistant Police Chief Ron Waldrop told the Dallas Morning News on November 6, 2000, "There's a conscious recognition of where eyewitness IDs have been wrong."

If that was true, then why has it taken those entrusted with seeing that justice is done so long to acknowledge a problem U.S Supreme Court Justice William Brennan knew existed three decades ago when he wrote, "The vagaries of eyewitness testimony are well known; the annals of criminal law are rife with the instances of mistaken identifications."

In a recent study conducted by "The Innocent Project" a New York organization dedicated to freeing the wrongful convicted, seventy-eight percent of the wrongful convictions they examined resulted from mistaken identifications.

Before moving into the individual factors that have been found to contribute to "mistaken identifications" a brief overview of the three step memory process: Acquisition, Retention and Retrieval and how it works is needed.

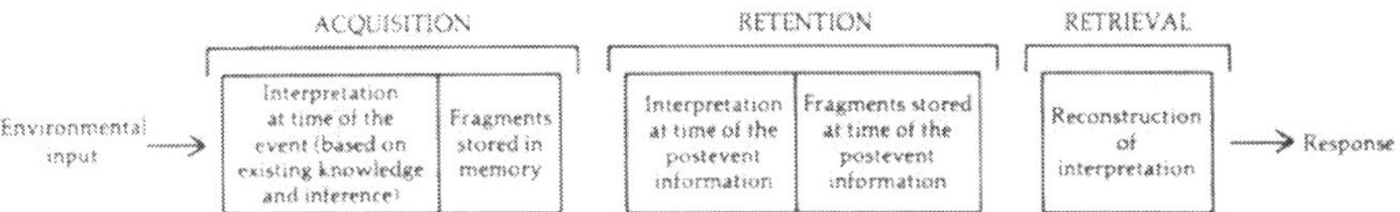

In order for a person to recall something, they first have to adequately perceive or acquire it. This requires that a certain amount of attention be paid to the initial stimulus. A failure of perception was likely what transpired in Voir Dire when Baldassano asked the jury pool to describe the bailiff. Chances were that those who couldn’t hadn't paid any attention to the man to begin with. For those potential jurors who didn't pay him any attention, it's doubtful they could recognize him under any circumstance. Another bailiff, the same race and body composition, could've filled in for the original one and those who didn't pay him any initial attention would hardly notice the difference.

Why? The image of the original bailiff was never adequately acquired therefore it left no lasting impression by which they could compare the two.

Another example of failure to perceive/acquire would be the mother of two rambunctious children, ages 8 and 10 who stopped by the corner store on her way home for a pack of cigarettes. Upon entering the store, she saw the vague image of someone in the store over by the beverages.

But her car was running and her kids were in the car, understandably that was where her focus was; she was trying to get in and out as quick as possible.

Later that night, while getting ready for bed, on the nightly news she hears the reporter say the store was robbed two hours earlier and the clerk was shot and killed. The police are looking for any potential witnesses who might have saw anything or anyone strange around the store. She thinks to herself she was in the store around that time and remembered someone else in there, most likely a man back by the beverages. Still, she can't identify who she saw in the store even though she was a few feet from them. Why?

She didn't adequately perceive the person. Her focus simply wasn't on them. This is how we can see and not see at the same time. To really see something or someone a conscious effort must be made.

At the perception/acquisition stage, there are two classes of phenomenon that affect a person's ability to adequately acquire and perceive information. Event factors and witness factors.

Event factors, such as exposure time-- how long a person has to view a phenomenon. The general premise is the longer a person has to view an event, the more accurate they recall it. Then there is what psychologist call, Detail Salience--which means that people perceive some details as more important than others. In a car wreck were the passenger is ejected through the windshield, people are more likely to recall details about the passenger and windshield then about the speed of car, type of car, or if it had any bump stickers. Our brains judge some facts more important than others. A third event factor is the level of violence involved in a incident.

The level of violence involved is particularly important for a case like the State of Texas vs. West.

Researchers Scott and Clifford (1978) conducted research to see if people perceived non violent and violent events the same way. Using forty eight test subjects, both male and female they found that individual's ability to adequately recall events involving violence was significantly reduced compared to their ability to recall non-violent events.

This was related to stress and exposure to violence either as victim or witness tended to be the ultimate stressor. Stress is considered a witness factor as it varies from one individual to the next, but the general consensus from the medical and scientific community was that the more stressed a person becomes the worse their perception becomes. Under extremely stressful situations people begin to have trouble with even mundane task such as spelling their own name.

The next leg of the stool involved in our attempts to recall information about a event we witness has been labeled the retention stage. It could be compared to the way a computer stores data for later use. However the problem with the file for humans is that it's not static, new information is constantly added and Delleted in a never ending often unconscious process.

For a innocent defendant the retention stage was the most dangerous because it's here that post event information is frequently induced. An example of post event information would be two bank tellers of a just robbed bank talking while they wait for the police to arrive. One teller tells the other, "my brother has an angel tattoo just like the one the guy had." But the other clerk didn't see the tattoo because she was too busy looking at the gun. Yet studies show that she will likely add it in her description of the robber that she gives to police, (Loftus 1975).

Researchers have even been able to show that objects that didn't exist at the time of the original event can be introduced into a witness's memory simply by the way a question is worded. In one study college students were shown a short film of a multi-car wreck caused by one car. A week after viewing the film they were asked one or two questions. The first was, "how fast was car “A” going when it ran the stop sign?" The second question was, "How fast was car “A” going when it turned right." Amazingly fifty-three percent of the students given the first question reported seeing the stop sign even though no stop sign existed.

What these studies show is that memories can be enhanced and even altered, simply by the way questions are worded. And the power to influence a witness's recollection is a dangerous tool in the hands of a eager frustrated detective who is convinced he has his man. This appears to be what happened with Lawrence Fields who in his original statement said the defendant had a hat on and got into a Suburban. However he changed his testimony on the witness stand.

When asked why/he said the detectives suggested it and he went with it."I don't remember caps because they asked me. They (homicide detectives) said anything on like their heads or stuff like that? I probably told him yeah, but I don't know."

This was an excellent example of how post event information can influence a witness, and it raises the question of what else the detectives suggested that witnesses agreed to even though it wasn't true?

The last factor related to the retention stage is the impact of non-verbal influences. (Hall et al.1978) demonstrated that a experimenters unstated expectations can affect how a research subject behaves. As previously stated the process by which police ask witnesses to identify a suspect from a photo-spread or live lineup is essentially an experiment conducted by the police. Because of the scientific communities recognition of how verbal and non-verbal influences can impact a subject they have been the main proponents behind the call for police departments to begin using double-blind experiment practices when conducting lineups.

In short any time after a witness witnesses an event, post event information can be induced.

The third leg of the stool of the 3 step memory process is the retrieval stage. This is where we attempt to correctly recall the information we originally acquired in stage one.

This stage has its own perils, one being the retrieval environment. A crime that takes place in a dark apartment complex's walkway is likely to be retrieved less accurately at the police station. Then there is the type of retrieval being utilized. One is the narrative form were a person is asked to tell what happened in their own words any way they like. This form of retrieval is more accurate but less thorough or complete, and important parts tend to get omitted.

The second form of retrieval is called the controlled narrative, and is the form most frequently employed by police investigating a crime. It involves multiple choice questions such as, "did the man have short or long hair? Was his skin rough looking or smooth?" While this form of retrieval tends to be more complete than the narrative or free form report, it's less accurate and the form most venerable to the abuses discussed earlier.

Individual Eyewitness Factors Involved In The West Case

It would take volumes to list and illustrate every factor that researchers have found contribute to mistaken identifications and the wrongful convictions that result from them.

In the West trial four major factors were involved:

1. The first was post event information the two eyewitnesses were together and left together.
2. The second was the long retention period, two months for Brown; three for Risher.
3. Then there was the phenomenon psychologists have labeled "Weapon Focus."
4. While the forth was unconscious transference.

Each of these is well documented in the annals of psychological literature in reference to eyewitness identifications. Taken separately each has the potential to lead to a mistaken identification. Collectively they likely led to Risher's and Brown's misidentification of the defendant as a shooter. The greatest disservice on the part of Don Irvin in his representation was not challenging the eyewitness testimony presented against his client on either of these scientific grounds, or presenting an expert who could.

Post Event Information and Enhanced Memory

Unlike Don Irvin, Baldassano had undoubtedly done his homework on the vagaries of eyewitness testimony. He knew that without independent witnesses who weren't connected to the victim, or each other he had a problem: Post Event Information.

Exactly how post event information works can be illustrated with the following example.

A man hears and sees a couple involved in a heated argument. He has no idea what the argument is about and since he can only hear bits and pieces, he can't tell one way or another. But a short while later, he overhears someone say the couple outside was arguing because the man had just caught the woman in bed with another man. This new information is unconsciously incorporated into the original memory of what he witnessed and organized in a logical way. After a few weeks if someone ask the man if he remembers the man and woman arguing outside the Burger King, he is likely to recall the argument along with the post event information he acquired, "Oh yeah, they were arguing because he caught her with another man." This happens without him realizing he has incorporated information into his memory he didn't actually hear or witness from the couple.

But what happens if the subsequent conversation he overheard was erroneous and the man and woman weren't arguing over infidelity but stolen money. The witness will swear he heard the argument and that it was about infiDellity never realizing how the additional post event information meshed with his original perception and crystallized into one memory.

Baldassano tried to deny the effect that post event information had on Brown and Risher. He asked them if they ever discussed the shooting and both repeatedly said they didn't talk about what they saw or who they saw do it. Such responses were the result of the prosecutor's pre-trial coaching.

It defies human logic that two friends riding in the same car will witness another friend, who one said he loved get killed and never discuss it, not that night or any other. Forget the fact that the following day Jessie Brown went to the man who was killed house.

Obviously they did discuss the shooting, more than likely quite extensively; that was the normal thing for them to do under the circumstances. What it meant for the defendant was that their memories of the event were transferred back and forth among each other. In such a scenario Risher's memory of the shooting would be enhanced and added to by Brown's and vice versa and because the process by which our memories are added to, or enhanced, is unconscious, neither would necessarily recognize it happening.

Under these circumstances, there weren't actually two eye witnesses against the defendant but one. And, if one was mistaken, this was likely passed on to the other. This was especially risky for the defendant because one of the witnesses Larry Risher said he knew the defendant by face. Leading to a situation where Risher possibly tried to describe who he thought did the shooting to Brown.

Had the state been able to produce one independent witness unconnected to Risher or Brown that could identify the defendant as a shooter, the threat of post event information and memory enhancement would've been minimized. But, without such a witness, it was likely that a misidentification by Risher, led to a misidentification by Brown or vice versa.

The Retention Interval

From the moment a person witnesses an event until they are called upon to recall it, is known as the retention interval. The longer the retention interval, the less accurate an event is recalled.

The grandfather of the study of how humans forget information over-time was Ebbinghaus (1885). He pioneered what has become known as the "Forgetting Curve," which shows that we forget quickly right after an event and then more gradually as time passes.

Since the days of Ebbinghaus, several follow up studies have been done by different researchers to test the accuracy of his theory. One by Sheppard (1967) tested how well a group of clerical workers could recognize pictures they viewed after two hours, three days, one week, and then four months. He found a hundred percent recognition after two hours but only a 57 percent recognition after four months. Being that there existed only two possible answers, yes they had seen the picture before or no, they hadn't.

A 57 percent recognition rate was only slightly better than if the participants had been merely guessing. With only two possible choices a person who had never viewed the original pictures still had a 50 percent chance of selecting the right one.

If Jessie Brown and Larry Risher had indeed witnesses the murder of their friend, left without discussing it, then didn't think about it or mention it until detective Abbondondolo showed up with a photo spread of the defendant two months later for Brown, and three for Risher, their memory of event would be severely compromised simply by the passage of time.

Assuming no post event information, memory enhancement, or undue police influence, Brown's ability to make a positive identification would've fallen significantly in the two months interval making it virtually impossible for him to make a positive identification the way the detective said he did.

Weapon Focus

Weapon focus can be described as the tendency of a crime victim, or witness of a violent crime to pay an inordinate amount of attention to the weapon, instead of the individual holding it. Thereby greatly reducing his or her ability to later recall other details, or identify the perpetrator.

Dr. Elizabeth Loftus, a expert in the field of eyewitness testimony testified in the California case, The People v. Garcia, about the effects of "Weapon Focus."

Q: Okay. Is the presence of a weapon a factor that is involved in how good or bad an eyewitness identification is?

A: Yes, it is. It's a factor and, in fact, the factor has been called "Weapon Focus," because what happens when a weapon is present is it tends to capture some of the witness's attention and some of the witness's processing time and capacity, leaving less time available for other details and other aspects of the incident, and this has the effect of reducing the ability to describe other details, although often people have a very good ability to describe the weapon. That's what is meant by weapon focus.

Q: Have there been studies on this to know why that is the case that people can identify the weapon?

A: Well, there is one study that was performed at Oklahoma State University within the last couple of years, showing that weapon focus did occur—that in a condition where there is a weapon present, people are good at remembering the weapon, but less good at remembering the person holding the weapon then in the corresponding controlled condition. However we don't have a very detailed understanding of why this occurs. Just that it does occur and probably has something to do with how much time the witness is spending on the weapon versus other details.

The research Dr. Loftus was referring to was conducted by (Johnson and Scott).In their study of witness's ability to later identify an individual they found that if a weapon was present individuals lost 70 percent of their ability to identify the person holding it, compared to those in the same study where no weapon was present.

There was strong evidence in the West case that, "Weapon focus," had occurred. At one point while Mr. Brown was on the witnesses stand for demonstration purposes, Baldassano produced a nine millimeter Taurus semi-automatic handgun. Mr. Brown had said he got a good look at the gun therefore Baldassano asked him:

Q: Does this look similar to the gun?

A: Yes

Science is often derided by critics for its emphasis on cold hard facts. But more and more the body of science seemed to be affirming what the defendant Kenneth West had been screaming sense his arrest, that he didn't shoot Sammie Ray Johnson.

In this instance the cold hard facts of science was saying that if Jessie Brown was focused on the weapon intently enough to testify about what it looked like, he couldn't have been focused on the shooters. There is no phenomenon called, "Weapon and Individual focus." The research was clear; if he was focused on one then he couldn't have been focused on the other.

This was why the defendant had been so adamant about getting Jessie Brown back on the witness stand.

He knew what he testified to was impossible—finally it appeared he had an irrefutable ally—science was saying the same thing.

Unconscious Transference

On a dark cloudy night a man robbed a railroad ticket clerk at gun point. Later that night downtown at the police station the clerk was shown a book of photos. Immediately he picked a young man from the photos as the man who had robbed him. But when the detectives went to arrest the man they ran into a brick wall. It turned out the man had an ironclad alibi. He was a sailor in the U.S Navy and had been out to sea on the day of the robbery. Ship records supported his story.

But the detectives wanted to know why the clerk had misidentified the man as the robber. In a follow-up investigation they discovered that the clerk picked the sailor because he looked familiar. It turned out the man was familiar, his Navy base was close by the railroad station and he had bought tickets from the clerk on previous occasions. However the clerk mistakenly assumed his recognition of the man was from the robbery, when in fact it was because the man had previously purchased tickets from him. This is a real life example of unconscious transference -- when a person seen or remembered in one setting is unconsciously transferred by the mind to another.

At California State University professor Buckhout wanted to see just how common this phenomenon was.

On the campus of CSU with 141 witnesses watching, he staged an assault on another professor by a deranged student. In the general proximity of the assault was an innocent bystander, who was the same age and race as the student-attacker. The staged assault took place in broad daylight and none of the 141 witnesses knew they were subjects in a study, or seeing a staged event; they thought they had actually witnessed a crime and quite a few were frighten and shook up following the incident.

A few weeks later as part of the alleged criminal investigation into the incident, the student-witnesses were shown photo-based lineups. Forty-percent of the students correctly chose the student who had actually attacked the professor, but another 25 percent chose the innocent bystander, a man who had simply witnessed the attack like they did but from a closer distance.

How could 25 percent of the witnesses pick an innocent man? Psychologist have labeled his phenomenon unconscious transference to refer to the process by which someone viewed in one situation is confused, or recalled as a person seen in a different situation.

Larry Risher testified he knew the defendant by sight as he had seen him at other clubs. On the night of the shooting, West was mingling around the parking lot and had walked past the line of cars slowly crawling out of the parking lot. When he heard the first gunshot and looked around, he estimated that he was at least fifty feet or more from where he thought the gunfire was coming from.

But as indicated by the research just by being in the parking lot when the shooting occurred he had a twenty-five percent chance of being erroneously identified as one of the shooters. This was compounded by Larry Risher, who seemed to have a minor obsession with the defendant and had paid him a significant amount of attention in the past, enough to know what kind of car he drove, even though they didn't know each other. If the defendant had walked past Risher right before the shooting, there was a good chance he still had the defendant's image in his mind when the shooting occurred as he ran behind the tire station such circumstances would be fertile ground for a case of unconscious transference to occur.

But even in the face of overwhelming evidence to the contrary, for most people seeing is believing. Therefore professor Buckhout wanted to teach the public a lesson about the shortcomings of eyewitness testimony that they would never forget.

To do this, he enlisted the help of NBC affiliate channel 4 in New York City. While watching the nightly news, viewers were shown what appeared to be a crystal clear surveillance tape of a robbery taking place. On the tape, a young man in a leather jacket lurked in the doorway of a well-lit hallway watching a unaware woman walk. Suddenly, he bolted from the doorway, snatched the woman's purse and knocked her to the ground in the process. From start to finish, the entire incident lasted twelve seconds. While making his escape, the robber ran, face forward, directly into the camera.

The tape ended and a six person lineup was plastered across the screen. Viewers were given a number and asked to call if they could identify the robber. Instantly the phone lines lit-up, the calls kept coming and coming until after 2,145 calls they unplugged the line.

In the lineup, the actually robber was in the number two position yet only seconds after watching the robbery, how many viewers identified the right man? Out of 2,145 viewers, only 14.3 percent correctly selected the right man; a mere 302 individuals. All the rest were wrong.

In a article entitled, "NEARLY 2000 EYEWITNESS CAN BE WRONG" professor Buckhout wrote, "The results were the same as if the witnesses were merely guessing, since on the basis of chance, we would expect only a 14.3 percent identification of any lineup participants, including number two."

The state of Texas sent Kenneth West to prison for life based on the testimony of two witnesses, but if 2000 witnesses can be wrong, couldn't two?

Chapter Nine - The Appeal

October 2nd, the day after he was banished from society, the defendant filed a notice of appeal and reaffirmed his desire to continue fighting his convictions by any means necessary. But he was off to a rocky start. The burden of fighting two murder charges had weighted his family down, mentally and emotionally, while exhausting every vestige of their savings. As a result, they were unable to afford any more legal representation and he was forced to file a pauper's oath and petition the court for a court appointed appeal attorney.

Apart from the financial strain, the defendant's mother, along with the rest of his family, was still in a state of shock - a 120 years. She couldn't believe it; he was barely 20 years old.

Throughout the trial, she had stood beside her son, although she knew the odds were stacked against young black men caught up in the jaws of the criminal justice system. Initially, she wanted to hire heavy weight Houston defense attorney Dick Degurin to represent her son. But after visiting with Mr. Degurin in his office, she quickly realized she could never afford to pay him. Nevertheless, it was on Degurin's recommendation that she ended up a floor above in, Don Irvin's office. However proximity was one thing; skills were another.

Nevertheless, she held a fair opinion of Don Irvin throughout the proceedings, but in the end, the squandered that goodwill. Her last impression of Don Irvin was of right after the judge sentenced her son to 120 years. He turned to her with a straight face and said, "I'm just glad they didn't give him life." Her jaw hit the floor; what else do you call a 120 years?

But she wasn't a quitter either and was more determined than ever to help her son. After talking to different attorneys following the trial, she found out they had a few dead months before the actual appeal got underway. Time for the court reporter to prepare the transcripts. This gave her a small window and she began scrapping together whatever money she could. And after taking out a second mortage on the modest three-bedroom home she had been living in for the past three decades, she landed on the door step of veteran appeal attorney Randy Schaffer.

Randy Schaffer had an impeccable reputation that he had earned by fighting tooth and nail for his clients. His name was on a short list of Houston appeal attorneys that also included Mac Secrest, Ken Mclean , Brain Wice, and Stanley Schenider along with a few others who had reputations for getting results. However, he warned her and her son that they were facing an uphill battle. The chances of winning an appeal in Texas regardless of the merits have grown increasingly slim. Beginning at the trial level conservative republicans dominated the bench.

In 2007, of the 21 filed district judgeships in Harris County, 19 were held by Republicans who were former prosecutors. At the appellate level, the deck was stack even worse. On the Court of Criminal Appeals, the state's highest appellant court, all nine judges were Republicans.

This didn't brood well for a criminal defendant. What it meant in a law and order state like Texas where being seen as tough on crime was synonymous with getting elected was that for all but the five percent of defendants who received a reversal the appellant courts were little more than rubber stamps. That sanctioned any and all decisions of the trial courts and prosecutors no matter how erroneous. Which was the reason so many Texas prosecutors were willing to ignore the law, the odds of a case getting overturned on appeal were slim to none, even when there was just cause.

But what was faith besides the substance of things hoped for? Stepping out on faith, the defendant began his decade-long fight in the appeal courts seeking the justice he was denied by the trial courts.

In the Carrington's case, he raised three grounds:

1. The introduction of the extraneous murder at the guilt or innocence phase denied him a fair trial and violated his rights.
2. The prosecutor used officer Thomas's to try to introduce improper and inadmissible evidence before the -jury.
3. Because he was not originally indicted under the law of parties it was a violation of his constitutional rights to have the law of parties added to the Jury charge.

In the Exxon case, the majority of the grounds the defendant challenged his conviction on centered on E. J. Van Buren's poor performance. He was ineffective on several grounds but specifically for:

1. Failing to request a jury instruction on defense of a third person
2. Failing to obtain a transcript of Jacoric Alexander's testimony prior to trial to be used for cross-examination purposes
3. Failing to call a material witness Alvando Ray in the guilt or innocence phase.
4. Failing to request a jury instruction on accomplice witness testimony as it related to St. Romain.

As expected, when the appeal court called upon Van Buren to answer the allegation against him, he filed an affidavit that said he was simply following the defendant's wishes and that was good enough for the courts.

For seven years the defendant's appeals made their way back and forth between different courts. Beginning in Houston at the 14th Court of Appeals, he journeyed to the Court of Criminal Appeals in Austin. Then it was back to the criminal courthouse.

Once it became apparent the state courts weren't going to listen, he traveled the few blocks to the Federal Courthouse. From there, it was onto New Orleans where he petitioned the Fifth Circuit Court of Appeals for redress when, once again, his pleas fell on deaf ears, he headed to Washington D.C, and the Supreme Court.

He went through two appellant attorneys on his legal odyssey until finally, unable to afford an attorney, he became his own lawyer filing legal petitions pro-se.

Throughout the Journey, two things never changed: The courts resistance nor his desire to continue fighting until he proved he was innocent.

Chapter Ten - Time To Grow

Throughout the ages, powerful men and sometimes women have stood in opposition of truth and justice. These are the Hitler's, Bull Conner's, Stalin's and George Wallace's of the world and our history books are rife with their deeds.

But, whether smothered by unjust authority or crushed to the ground beyond recognition, like justice, truth is a force onto itself and like the mythical Phoenix; it has a way of rising again and again. If the truth had one requirement it would be the same as a small child, time to grow.

Following the defendant's conviction that child began to grow at a robust clip as new information flowed into the defendant's camp. Information the jury never heard due to the lazy effort of the defendant's attorney; an effort whose hallmark was very little pretrial investigation. This failure, coupled with the prosecutor's and homicide detectives' systematic effort to ignore any and all information unfavorable to the state, resulted in the defendant's wrongful conviction.

In his conviction for the death of Sammie Johnson, the state had surmised that the defendant went into a crowded nightclub parking lot with fifteen hundred people and murdered Mr. Johnson, a total stranger, for no apparent reason.

As this case was the most suspect, it was inevitably the first to unravel. During his trial, the defendant was concerned with why there weren't any other witnesses besides the deceased's two friends, who were later discovered to have played a larger role in the ordeal then they initially revealed.

But it turned out there were other witnesses; a lot of them. First there was a man named Melvin Sanders who had been in the parking lot on the night of the shooting.

Mr. Sanders was walking by the victims' car at the time of the shooting and was struck in the foot by a stray bullet. Following the shooting, he left the scene but later contacted detectives who were unaware of his ordeal. However, it turned out that Mr. Sanders wasn't a stranger to the police; he had several previous run-ins with the Houston Police department. His own criminal past provided him a strong incentive not to get involved and he told the detective he didn't see anything.

What was interesting was that the detectives accepted this and didn't do any follow ups with him to impress upon him the, "seriousness of the offense," in order to get him to come forward with information he may have had. The way detective Abby testified he did with Jessie Brown who was equally reluctant to get involved.

Nevertheless, it was discovered after the trial that Mr. Sanders had discussed the incident and made statements that the defendant wasn’t one of the assailants who he saw shoot and kill Mr. Johnson and that could've been used to exonerate the defendant.

By failing to conduct a thorough pre-trial investigation, and by not appreciating the anti-police/anti-witness culture that prevails in much of the inner city black community, a result of years of abuse and mistreatment at the hands of the police department, Don Irvin dropped the ball. Had he properly deposed Mr. Sanders, it was more than likely his testimony would've been extremely beneficial to the defendant. Instead, he was never even interviewed by the defense.

The pattern of neglect repeated itself with Eric Laws and his friend Victor Simon. When the shooting happened, they were cruising in Mr. Law's Cadillac when the car was suddenly struck by the victim's Dellta 88. Because of the wreck, Mr. Laws and Mr. Simon remained at the scene and gave statements to detective, which was basically that they didn't see the shooting, or who did it. For these two gentlemen, this was the simplest way not to get involved and no one ever pressed either of them on their lack of recollection. In fact, there was no need to. The prosecutor already had two witnesses with a personal stake in the outcome which made them extremely amendable/pro-prosecution witnesses. Yet no reasonable explanation could be found for Don Irvin's failure to contact, let alone interview, these two crucial witnesses.

Two years after the defendant's conviction, another piece of post trial information was discovered. This one concerned Yattie Gordon, the other man riding in the black Impala with Risher and Brown. Durning the trial, it was more than a little strange that Mr. Gordon wasn't called by the state to testify. The general rule was that if the state didn't do something, there was a good reason they didn't. So, what was their reason for excluding Yattie Gordon from the trial?

According to Jessie Brown, he was standing outside the car with Larry Risher and Yattie Gordon when the shooting happened; therefore, Mr. Gordon would've been in as good of position as Brown and Risher to witness what took place in the Carrington's parking lot.

The information that came to light surfaced after Mr. Gordon discussed the shooting with a friend of his. According to Mr. Gordon, he was with Larry Risher and Jessie Brown in the club parking lot drinking prescription cough syrup and smoking weed. They had also taken some Xanax and smoked PCP earlier in the evening. When the shooting started, they were in the process of passing around a cigar filled with marijuana and were more in the car than out of it in a effort to keep the smoke out of sight in case any police were in the area.

Because of this, Larry Risher was the only one of the trio who thought he saw the shooter and when they were on their way home, he kept saying, "that fat nigga who be in all the clubs was out there."

This was consistent with what the defense already knew - that the three friends had discussed the shooting extensively. However, what no one outside of the men in the Impala knew at the time of the defendant's trial was what transpired in the seconds following the shooting.

After the shooting Jessie Brown ran across the street to check on his friends who had been shot. But Risher and Gordon drove over in the Impala and parked in the lot behind the Stop N Go. In addition to the turmoil from the shooting, the men in the blue Dellta 88 panicked because they had something in their car that they didn't want to get caught with when the police arrived who would be there at any second. That something was a large wood and black SKS Assault rifle that one of the men wrapped in a shirt and stashed behind the store next to the dumpsters. In an effort to keep their friends from getting caught with the gun, Larry Risher pulled his car by the dumpster and put the assault rifle in his truck. Later that night, he gave the gun to Jessie Brown who returned it to Jerome Sampson the next day.

The information Mr. Gordon told his friend was the Holy Grail. It put all the messing pieces together. For starters, it explained why the trio, who had just watched their friend murdered, left as soon as the police arrive. It turned out they were worried that someone may have seen them get the gun and didn't want to risk it. It also explains why both Larry Risher and Jessie Brown sought to avoid the police in the weeks and months following the shooting.

Another bombshell surfaced concerning Mr. Risher. On the witness stand, he came across as a squeaky clean young man who said he didn't even drink; yet, Mr. Gordon, who had an extensive criminal record, asserted that they had been doing drugs in the interval before the shooting and his statement refuted that. And it was later discovered, that Mr. Risher was a major drug dealer in the Acres Homes area of Houston who was responsible for trafficking hundreds of pounds of cocaine and that Mr. Gordon worked for him in his drug business.

Had the jury been privileged to know that the state's two ID witnesses obstructed justice and tampered with evidence by removing their friend's gun from the scene, it was very likely they would've taken a closer look at their testimony. It would've further destroyed the prosecutor's "innocent victim theory," as innocent victims don't ride around with assault rifles in their car.

Nevertheless, the jury never learned of this information nor did they have a chance to hear from Melvin Sanders, Eric Law, or Victor Simons, three witnesses who could've exonerated the defendant.

They also didn't see the surveillance tapes from the surrounding businesses that showed the large crowds and bumper to bumper traffic in the parking lot on the night of the shooting. Although there exists enough evidence to prove the defendant didn't kill Sammie Ray Johnson on the night of June 6, 1997, no courts have ever seriously considered his innocent claims.

When it was all said and done, he finally understood what the old convict was telling him when he said, "They don't play fair." It's not about justice, but convictions.

He was up against the same “convict at all cost injustice machine” that had already sent over 250 DNA-proven innocent men to prison for decades for crimes they didn't commit; 43 of them from Texas.

But the truth of the matter is that from the first time Kenneth West entered the 176th Courtroom, he faced a loaded deck. Number one, he was young, black, and unemployed, which meant that he not only fit the profile of a street criminal, but also bore the characteristic that most Americans view synonymous with danger. These factors made it nearly impossible for him to be tried by a jury of his peers. They further made it doubtful that any of the middle class college educated professionals in the courtroom in charge of his fate could empathize with him or see his humanity.

The second disadvantage that undoubtedly played a significant role in his wrongful conviction was that he was poor. In America no money means nobody cares. No high powered lawyers. No news coverage. No nothing. Justice may be blind, but it has never been free.

In the end Kenneth West received the only form of justice available to poor, racial minorities, particularly in Harris County. Injustice.

Appendixes

Appendix 1- Witness Statements

HOUSTON POLICE DEPARTMENT
Homicide Division
WITNESS STATEMENT
County of Harris State of Texas
Date: Thursday, June 12, 1997 Time: 1018 Hrs.

Before me, the undersigned authority, this day, personally appeared Jerome Sampson, believed by me to be a credible person, who after being sworn upon his/her oath, did depose and say:

My name is Jerome Sampson. I am a black male and I am 19 years old, having been born 10-12-77. My home address is ____________________ and my home telephone number is ________________. I can also be reached by calling _____________. My Texas driver's license number is ____________________ and my Social Security number is __________ . I have attained 12 years of formal education. I am unemployed at this time.

I am at the Homicide Division of the Houston Police Department to make a statement regarding the shooting I was in. Just after midnight on Friday, June 6, 1997 I arrived at Carrington's club on Main Street. I was with my friends, Robert Levi, Carl Anderson, and Sammie Johnson. I was in the car and I was sitting behind the steering wheel. I was driving the car and I own the car. Sammie was sitting behind me in the back seat. Carl was sitting in the front passenger seat, and Robert was sitting in the rear passenger seat.

Before I got to the club I was at my house and I left to go pick those other guys up. I drove from my house to Pecan Shadows on Parker Road and I Picked up all three guys. We left from there and to the gas station at Parker and Yale and then drove to the parking lot of Carrington's.

When we got to Carrington's I pulled in off of main. I entered the parking lot somewhere in the middle of the parking lot. I drove towards the middle of the shopping center and it was real crowded. There were also too many people and cars in the parking lot. I stopped the car and parked in the parking lot because someone ahead of me stopped. All of us got out of the car and we sat on the car. While we were sitting there we saw a friend whose nick name is "Bald Head." We talked to him for a little while and he was there with us for about five minutes. The girls that were in the car ahead of us came back and they drove away. I think they were in a Mazda 929, but I don't know these girls.

Once the car in front of us moved we got back in the car and I drove to leave the parking lot. I drove through the parking lot toward the store and then made a left and went through a driveway in the parking lot. I was driving slow and I saw some guys come around both the front and back of my car. The traffic was already slow so I didn't have to stop for them.

I didn't pay too much attention to them because I don't have a beef with anybody. As I was driving I saw some more friends who were outside their car. One of these guy's name was Bull. Bull drives a new maroon impala SS. I waived to him and he waived back. I passed him and then I heard the shooting. I had my music turned up loud while we were driving.

Before the shooting had started I saw a red Lincoln in the parking lot. It was the older kind that is like a box. I saw this car as it was coming in the parking lot, it was coming towards me. I saw two black guys in the car as it was coming toward me and he had pulled to the right. This car was stopped when we went passed it. I didn't see anyone get out of the car

I saw my front windshield get a big hole in it and then I turned to look around, but something told me to get down and I did. I smashed on the gas and Sammie had slumped over in his seat. I guess they thought that he had just ducked and that's when they fired into my seat. I never looked up as my car went forward, I had my head down. My friend Robert Levi told me that they were still shooting as the car went across the street.

My car came to a stop and I thought my car hit the store. I looked at the guys in the car with me, then got out of the car and looked in the parking lot. I saw that the red Lincoln was gone. It could have been burgundy or red. Then I walked into the stop and go store.

I was taken to the hospital by ambulance. I had been shot once in the right back below my shoulder. The bullet is still in me and the doctor is going to talk to me about getting it out.

I looked at the pictures in the booklet you gave me and I am sure about the guy in position number five. I didn't see him with a gun, but he was in the parking lot close to me. This was right before the shooting started. He was behind me near a suburban and the suburban was maroon or a dark color. In fact, I think he was wearing the same shirt that night that he has in the picture. I'm not so sure, but I think the guy in spot #2 was there also can't be so sure about him.

Dell Robinson

I have read this, my statement, consisting of two pages and find it to be true and correct to the best of my knowledge.

signature

notary public

1133 6-12-97

HOUSTON POLICE DEPARTMENT
Homicide Division
WITNESS STATEMENT
County of Harris State of Texas
Date: Thursday, June 12, 1997 Time: 1002 Hrs.

Before me, the undersigned authority, this day, personally appeared LAWRENCE FREEMAN FIELDS, believed by me to be a credible person, who after being sworn upon his/her oath, did depose and say:

My name is LAWRENCE FREEMAN FIELDS. I am a BLACK MALE and I am 19 years old, having been born 9-9-77. My home address is _________________ and my home telephone number is __________ . I can also be reached by calling _____________. My TX driver's license number is _____________ and my Social Security number is ________. I have attained 12 years of formal education. I am employed by KROGER. My work address is 3216 BRAESWOOD and my work telephone number is 555-6800.

THIS PAST THURSDAY NIGHT, FRIDAY MORNING, I WAS WITH A FRIEND NAMED TRACY GRAVETT. AT ABOUT 2:00 AM WE WERE GOING TO GO TO THE JACK IN THE BOX RESTAURANT ON MAIN. WE GOT CAUGHT UP IN THE TRAFFIC FROM THE PEOPLE TRYING TO GET OUT OF CARRINGTONS. WE WERE IN TRACY'S CAR, I WAS IN THE FRONT PASSENGER SEAT, AND TRACY WAS DRIVING. WE WERE WAITING FOR ABOUT 5 MINUTES AND TRACY LOOKED OVER AND SAW PEOPLE RUNNING. THAT'S WHEN I HEARD THE GUNSHOTS.

TRACY WAS SAYING' "OH, MY GOD THEY'RE SHOOTING, THEY'RE SHOOTING". THEN TRACY DUCK DOWN IN MY

LAP. I LEANED BACK IN THE CHAIR, BUT I COULD NOT GET THE CHAIR BACK. SO I LEANED OVER TRACY AND PUT MY HANDS ON THE DASH. THEN I LOOKED UP AND I SAW THE CAR COMING TOWARD US. THEY DIDN'T STOP SHOOTING UNTIL THE CAR GOT OUT OF THE PARKING LOT AND INTO THE STREET. THEN TRACY LOOKED UP AND SAID, THEY'RE GONNA HIT US". THEN TRACY LEANED OVER AGAIN AND I LEANED OVER AGAIN. THAT'S WHEN THE CAR HIT US.

WHEN THEY HIT US THE CAR WENT UP THE SIDEWALK TOWARD THE SIDE OF THE STOP & GO. IT DRUG US UP THERE WITH IT AND HIT US AGAIN. THEN I GOT OUT OF THE CAR AND I RAN TO THE BACK OF THE STOP AND GO. I WAS GOING TO TRY TO GO TO THE BURGER KING. THEN I WENT BACK TO GET TRACY. THAT'S WHEN I SAW ONE OF THE GUYS WHO GOT SHOT IN THE BACK. HE HAD WENT TO THE BACK OF THE STOP & GO AND KEPT GOING AROUND THE CORNER. THEN I WENT TO THE CAR AND I SAW THAT THE CAR WAS ALL SHOT UP, AND THERE WAS A GUY IN THE BACK SEAT. THEN I WENT AROUND THE CAR TO GET TRACY.

TRACY GOT OUT OF THE CAR AND WENT TO THE PHONE. THAT'S WHEN ME AND TWO OTHER GUYS TRIED TO CALL 911. AFTER I CALLED 911 I WENT BACK TO THE CAR AND THEN CALLED MY UNCLE. A SECURITY GUARD CAME AROUND THERE AND 'TOOK THE PHONE. I WENT BACK TO THE CAR TO GET THE KEYS AND TRACY'S PURSE. THEN A GUY WHO WAS SITTING IN ANOTHER CAR WHEN THE SHOOTING HAPPENED WAS BY THE CAR THAT GOT SHOT. HE WAS TRYING TO GET THE GUY IN THE BACK SEAT OF

THE CAR TO SIT UP. SO THEN BY THAT TIME I THINK 3 OR 4 POLICE CARS CAME. THEY WERE TRYING TO GET EVERYBODY TO LEAVE AND TO GET AWAY. EVERYBODY CLEARED UP. THREE POLICEMEN GOT THE GUY OUT OF THE BACK SEAT AND LAID HIM ON THE GROUND. BY THAT TIME MY UNCLE CAME.

I SAW TWO GUYS ON THE SIDE OF THE CAR SHOOTING. THEY WERE STANDING BY A SUBURBAN THAT WAS BEHIND THE CAR. THEY WERE SHOOTING INTO THE BACK OF THE CAR. ONE OF THEM WAS TALL AND HEAVY. THE OTHER WAS SHORTER AND THIN. BOTH OF THEM HAD ON DARK PANTS AND CAPS. THE HEAVY GUY WAS DARK SKINNED. THE SHORT ONE WAS A LITTLE BRIGHTER. WHEN THE SHOOTING STOPPED AND EVERYBODY STARTED RUNNING THE TWO GUYS GOT INTO A SUBURBAN AND DROVE OFF TOWARD KIRBY. THE SUBURBAN WAS DARK, LIKE A BLUE. IT LOOKED NEW. THE WINDOWS WERE TINTED, SO I DON'T KNOW HOW MANY OTHER PEOPLE WERE INSIDE.

I DON'T KNOW WHAT THE SHOOTING WAS ABOUT.

I have been informed that under the PENAL CODE of the STATE OF TEXAS, Section 37.02: A person commits the offense of PERJURY if, with intent to deceive and with knowledge of the statement's meaning; he/she makes a false statement under oath or swears to the truth of a false statement previously made; and the statement is required or authorized by law to be made under oath.

Dell Robinson

I have read this, my statement, consisting of 2 page/pages, and find it to be true and correct to the best my knowledge as typed by Sgt. K. E. Vachris.

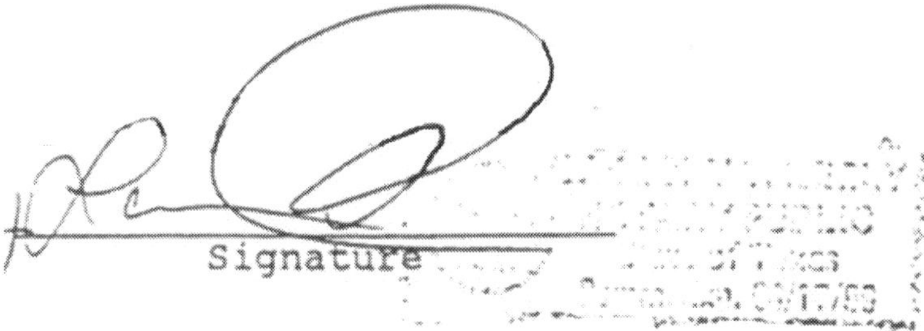

Subscribed and sworn to before me, the undersigned authority on Thursday, June 12, 1997

Notary Public 10:22 hrs 6-12-97

End of statement of LAWRENCE FREEMAN FIELDS taken on PC2 (LAWRENCE).

HOUSTON POLICE DEPARTMENT
Homicide Division
WITNESS STATEMENT
County of Harris State of Texas
Date: Monday, June 9, 1997 Time: 1145 Hrs.

Before me, the undersigned authority, this day, personally appeared TRACIE DIONNE GRAVETT, believed by me to be a credible person, who after being sworn upon his/her oath, did depose and say:

My name is TRACIE DIONNE GRAVETT. I am a BLACK FEMALE and I am 21 years old, having been born 8-25-75. My home address is ____________________ and my home telephone number is _________. I can also be reached by calling _____________. My CA driver's license number is ________________ and my Social Security number is _______________. I have attained 14 years of formal education. I am employed by KROGER. My work address is S. BRAESWOOD AT KIRBY and my work telephone number is 713-555-6800.

LAST THURSDAY NIGHT, ACTUALLY FRIDAY MORNING, AT ABOUT 1:45 AM I WAS IN THE MIDDLE OF WESTRIDGE WAITING FOR THE LIGHT TO CHANGE AT S. MAIN. THERE WAS A LOT OF TRAFFIC FROM CARRINGTON CLUB. I WAS WITH MY FRIEND LAWRENCE FIELDS. LAWRENCE AND I WERE GOING TO THE TACO BELL.

WHILE I WAS SITTING IN THE TRAFFIC WAITING FOR THE LIGHT TO CHANGE I HEARD GUNSHOTS. THE GUNSHOTS SOUNDED LIKE THEY WERE IN THE PARKING LOT BETWEEN THE ARBY'S AND THE TIRE STORE. I LOOKED OVER AND SAW A CAR FACING ME BUT STOPPED IN THE

PARKING LOT WHERE CARRINGTONS IS LOCATED. I ALSO SAW THREE BLACK MALES STANDING BEHIND THE CAR. THEY WERE ALL SHOOTING AT THE CAR. TWO OF THE MEN WERE BEHIND THE CAR AND ONE WAS ON THE PASSENGER SIDE BY THE BACK WINDOW. ALL THREE WERE SHOOTING. WHEN I SAW THEM SHOOTING I DUCKED DOWN IN LAWRENCE'S LAP. LAWRENCE DUCKED DOWN OVER ME. LAWRENCE LOOKED UP AND SAW THE CAR COMING TOWARD US. THEN I REMEMBER MY CAR BEING HIT ON THE FRONT LEFT SIDE. THE IMPACT SPUN US AROUND. WHEN I GOT UP I SAW THAT I WAS ON THE CURB. I DON'T KNOW HOW I GOT UP ON THE CURB.

LAWRENCE GOT OUT OF THE CAR AND TOLD ME TO GET OUT. I TURNED OFF THE CAR AND GOT OUT. THEN I RAN OVER TO THE STOP AND GO TO THE PAY PHONES. I CALLED A FRIEND.

ONE OF THE MEN SHOOTING WAS WEARING A WHITE T-SHIRT. THEY ALL APPEARED TO BE PRETTY TALL. I ONLY SAW THEM FOR A MOMENT AND THEY WERE PRETTY FAR AWAY.

I have read the above portion of this, my statement, and to be true and correct to the best of my knowledge.

I have been informed that under the PENAL CODE of the STATE OF TEXAS, Section 37.02: A person commits the offense of PERJURY if, with intent to deceive and with knowledge of the statement's meaning; he/she makes a false statement under oath or swears to the truth of a false statement previously made; and the statement is required or authorized by law to be made under oath.

I have read this, my statement, consisting of 2 page/pages, and find it to be true and correct to the best of my knowledge as typed by Sgt. K.E. Vachris.

GREGORY T. [illegible]
NOTARY PUBLIC
State of Texas
Comm. Exp. [illegible]

Signature

Notary Public

12 noon 6-9-77

GREGORY T. [illegible]
NOTARY PUBLIC
State of Texas
Comm. Exp. [illegible]

Signature

Notary Public

12 noon 6-9-77

HOUSTON POLICE DEPARTMENT
Homicide Division
WITNESS STATEMENT
County of Harris State of Texas
Date: Friday, June 6, 1997 Time: 603 Hrs.

Before me, the undersigned authority, this day, personally appeared Tanicka Michelle Robins, believed by me to be a credible person, who after being sworn upon his/her oath, did depose and say:

My name is Tanicka Michelle Robins. I am a Black female and I am 20 years old, having been born March 09, 1977. My home address is ____________________ and my home telephone number is _________. My Texas driver's license number is ________________ and my Social Security number is ___________. I have attained 12 years of formal education. I am employed by Rainbo Kids Store. My work address is Sharpstown Mall and my work telephone number is (713)555-5440.

At about 2:00 am, I was sitting in the car with two of my friends named Jamie and Dee. We were parked at the Arby's restaurant parking lot on South Main. The parking lot was jammed with traffic, so we were just trying to get out to go home. All of a sudden, I heard a lot of gunshots coming from one of the exits. I saw a chubby Black male, brown skinned, with a low hair cut and bushy eyebrows. He was wearing a striped white and blue shirt and white jeans. He was wearing the new black and white Air Jordan tennis shoes. He looked young and looked to be in his early 20s. I saw him raising his shirt and he had what appeared to be a black gun. He bent over slightly as he ran.

Everybody immediately hit the ground. He ran from the drive thru area to the back of the parking lot, headed in the direction of South Main. He ran in the direction of where two long limousines had been parked earlier. I noticed that there were about fifteen people in it earlier. He may have ran to one of those limousines. When I looked for the limousine, it was gone. One of the limousines had left before the shooting had happened. There was a short, slim, dark, Black male that was walking behind him. He was wearing black shorts and some type of red and blue striped polo type shirt. He had on red and black colored Jordan tennis shoes. He was real thin and his face looked sunked in. He was about 16 to 17 years old.

There was another male walking behind those two, but I don't think he was with them. I did not pay much attention to him. I heard that a guy had gotten shot and was dead, but I did not see him. I heard at least 20 shots and it sounded like they were having a shootout. The guys that got shot were in a large four dour blue vehicle. It appeared that they wrecked into a Stop-N Go store and a black Volkswagen Jetta struck their car. The males I saw were not coming from the direction where I heard the gunshots. I think I might be able to recognize the males again if I saw them.

I have been informed that under the PENAL CODE of the STATE OF TEXAS, Section 37.02: A person commits the offense of PERJURY if, with intent to deceive and with knowledge of the statement's meaning; he/she makes a false statement under oath or swears to the truth of a false statement previously made; and the statement is required or authorized by law to be made under oath.

I have read this, my statement, consisting of 2 page/pages, and find it to be true and correct to the best of my knowledge as typed by E. Gonzalez.

Signature

Subscribed and sworn to before me, the undersigned authority on Friday, June 6, 1997.

Notary Public

Appendix 2- People vs Garcia

In the case of the People vs. Garcia, a California case, Dr. Elizabeth F. Loftus a psychological expert in the field of "Eye Witness" testimony was called upon by the defense to testify to the various factors that can effect "Eye Witness," testimony.

The Garcia case involves a Hispanic defendant Jose Garcia who was accused of killing a store clerk during a robbery. The state's entire case against him rested on the testimony of two eye-witnesses, thus providing a strong parallel with the West case.

An excerpt of Dr. Loftus testimony in the Garcia case as it relates to eyewitness testimony has been reprinted here. It sheds light on the nature of eye witness testimony and what the current body of research has to say about its' peculiarities. Second it highlights the essence of what a expert witness in the field of eye witness testimony would've added to West's defense and the jury's understanding of the various problems frequently associated with eye witness testimony.

Q. I would like to ask you whether or not there are certain factors that may affect eyewitness identification in the case of People v. Garcia. Do you understand what I'm saying?

A. Yes

Q. All right. First, the retention interval; you mentioned that earlier in your discussion with Mr. Harry, also. Can you explain for me what that is?

A. Yes. The retention interval is simply the period of time between a crime or some other incident and a witness's recollection of that incident.

Q. Are there any studies in that particular area?

A. There are many studies which looked at the effects of varying the length of the retention interval.

Q. And have psychologist reached any conclusion in that area?

A. Yes, they have.

Q. Can you tell me what those are?

A. Well, if I could use the paper? If you look at -- this is the conclusion that psychologist have reached about the relationship between memory and the retention interval. The function between these two is a negatively decelerating function. That means it drops off quite rapidly at first and then the decay is much more gradual. And this was first discovered by Ebbinghaus in 1885. It's called the forgetting curve and it's been replicated in laboratories across the country with different kinds of materials and different kinds of witnesses. And what this basically says is that we remember much less after a long retention interval than after a shorter one.

Q. So what it generally says is as time goes by you forget. Is that right?

A. Well, in simple terms, yes.

Q. But you also forget in a particular manner. You forget more at a particular stage and less at another stage?

A. That's correct.

Q. Okay. Thank you. What about the factors of stress? Do you know what I mean by that?

A. Yes

Q. What does that mean?

A. Well, stress is typically used to-- there are different definitions of stress that are used by psychologist, but it commonly means the feeling of being aroused, afraid, upset. That's a popular use of the term "stress." There are much more technical definitions.

Q. Does it have a meaning in relation to eyewitness identification?

A. Well, yes it does, because there is a relationship between stress and memory or eyewitness ability.

Q. Can you describe what that relationship is?

A. Yes. I will use the diagram.

Q. Would you use a new sheet of paper?

A. Again, while the relationship between memory and stress is somewhat more complex, this is memory or any sort of cognitive performance, and this is stress or fear or arousal, the relationship is an inverted U-shape function and this is called the Yerkes-Dodson law, named after the two psychologists who discovered it in 1908.What this is saying is that under very high stress or fear or arousal and also under very, very low stress, such as when you are just waking up in the morning, we are less good rememberers and perceivers than we are under ordinary optimal moderate levels of stress.

Q. Which means when you are nice and wide awake, you are remembering the best. Is that correct?

A. That's true. And up here you can imagine if you have just gotten into an auto accident or something very stressful and upsetting that happened to you, you wouldn't want to sit down and start to try to work a crossword puzzle or do something that required some concentration.

Q. What you mean in relation to memory is, this is like the better memory as we go up the line, right?

A. That's true.

Q. And with high stress or very low stress, memory is going to be at the lower level or not as good. Is that what you are saying?

A. That's correct.

Q. Okay. Is the presence of a weapon a factor that is involved in how good or bad an eyewitness identification is?

A. Yes, it is. It's a factor and, in fact, the factor has been called "weapon focus," because what happens when a weapon is present is it tends to capture some of the witness's attention and some of the witness's processing time and capacity, leaving less time available for other details and other aspects of the incident, and this has the effect of reducing the ability to describe other details, although, often, people have a very good ability to describe the weapon. That's what is meant by weapon focus.

Q. Have there been studies on this to know why that is the case that people can identify the weapon?

A. Well, there is one study that was performed at Oklahoma State University with the last couple of years, showing that weapon focus did occur— that in a condition where there is a weapon present, people are good at remembering the weapon, but less good at remembering the person who was holding the weapon than in the corresponding controlled condition. However, we don't have a very detailed understanding of why this occurs. Just that it does occur and it probably has something to do with how much time the witness is spending on the weapon versus the other details.

Q. That's a "probably." Can you say that with any amount of certainty?

A. No. I think, actually, it would be possible to do it if you had an experiment in which you could measure eye movement patterns, but it hasn't been done with that sophisticated equipment.

Q. What do you mean by "measure eye movement patterns"? What does that have to do?

A. That the experiment I just described in which it was shown that a condition in which a weapon was present caused people to focus on the weapon and look at other details less often. We only know that because we look at their final reports. We ask them questions at the very end and they can remember the weapon very well, but they don't remember the faces as well. To really know that that is because they were focusing on the weapon, it would be nice to have a study in which you recorded eye movements- there is equipment which you can use which allows you to see where people are looking, but this is very fancy and expensive equipment and it's not available for most of the scientific studies where it would be nice to have it.

A. Yes

Q. But that doesn't necessarily mean people are focusing in on the weapon?

A. We assume they are, because they remember the weapon later and there is a detriment in their ability to remember other details.

Q. In regard to stress and weapon focus, those factors, have you heard the statement involved in-- a statement by an eyewitness in a stressful situation:"I will never forget that face?"

MR.HARRY: Object to this, your Honor; calls for something that the witness has no expertise on. She hasn't conducted such an experiment with people involved in a holdup.

THE COURT: Well, Mr. Harry, I think she has indicated earlier that she has conducted experiments intended to obtain the kind of information that you can obtain about what might be involved in the identification process as a result of such an experience. Now, are you saying that the only way you can obtain information about what happens when something occurs is to have the exact same thing occur? I mean, is that the basis?

MR.HARRY: That's not what I'm saying.

THE COURT: Okay. Mr .Christensen, can you rephrase that question somehow?

MR.CHRISTENSEN: Q. Well, let's see. Has it been shown in the studies that you have read about or conducted yourself and your readings in the area, that a statement under stressful condition, "I will never forget that face," has it been shown whether or not that would be a valid or invalid statements?

MR.HARRY: Your Honor, I would object. She has not said that she has conducted any experiments where people say-

MR.CHRISTENSEN: She is an expert for reading-

THE COURT: Why don't you ask Dr. Loftus whether in her experience with all these experiments she has conducted, some people tend to overrate their identification. Isn't that the point?

MR.CHRISTENSEN: Yes. In particular, in regards to stress, yes.

THE COURT: All right.

MR.CHRISTENSEN: Q. The question has already been stated. Can you give me an answer?

A. Yes. People do overrate their identification, partly because they don't understand the operation of stress and how it affects memory.

Q. Have you heard about a concept called "post event information"?

A. Yes.

Q. Big word.

A. Yes.

Q. What does it mean?

A. Post event information simply refers to information that is presented in some way to a witness after a to-be-remembered event is completely over.

Q. And has that been studied by psychologist, the effects that may have on a subsequent identification?

A. Yes, it has.

Q. In fact, you have indicated a study you have recently done yourself. Is that correct?

A. That's correct.

Q. Is there a particular result that you have reached?

A. In the experiments which studied post event information, they have found that people will take this information that comes in during the retention interval, as that information about the barn came in during the retention interval in one of my experiments. They will take this information and integrate it into their memories, either supplementing their memory or altering or adding to their memories, and it now becomes, in a sense, a part of their recollection. Now, what percentage of the people do this depends completely on other factors: how good a look the witness got at what is going to be remembered; how convincing the post event information is. But it can come in a number of different ways. You saw an experiment, or I described an experiment, in which it came in during questioning.

It can also come in during the course of overhearing a conversation or engaging in a conversation or reading a newspaper article. And information supplied in this way can become a part of a witness's memory and a witness can be very confident about--very confident that the witness actually saw what the witness has only heard about.

Q. Or seen somewhere else other than at the time it happened?

A. Well, that's true, too.

Q. Does this get back to the fact that the brain is again, not a video--memory is not videotaped?

A. Well, the studies involving this factor, nice examples of how you can take information from different sources and even from different modalities. In one case you are actually seeing the events, but you are hearing or reading a piece of post event information and you take this information or we all take this information, integrate it together to produce something that is different from what we actually, ourselves experience.

Q. Again, that has been studied over a period of time?

A. Yes.

Q. "Unconscious transference," does that mean anything to you?

A. Yes. That's a term which means the mistaken recollection or the confusion of a person seen in one situation with a person that has been seen in a different situation or in a different context. And that definition is somewhat confusing and I can best explain what it means by using an example from Patrick Wall's book — the book is called Eyewitness Identification in Criminal Cases. Mr. Wall brings up an example of a train clerk who was robbed. I believe it was at gunpoint. The train clerk subsequently went to a lineup and picked a sailor out of the lineup. The sailor did not commit the robbery, had a very good alibi, but had purchased tickets from this train clerk on three prior occasions. So you can see what is happening in this situation. The train clerk, the witness, goes to the lineup. In fact, there is a face in the lineup that looks familiar and that familiarity is mistakenly related back to the crime, rather than back to the purchasing of tickets where it properly belongs. That's a classic example of unconscious transference.

Q. Other than Mr. Wall's example, has that concept been studied?

A. Yes, it has.

Q. And what result reached?

A. Well, the major thing we know from the experiments on unconscious transference is that it is a real phenomenon and you can produce it in a controlled laboratory situation. That people will look at faces that they have seen at different times in different contexts and mistakenly relate those faces back to an incorrect situation.

Q. Thank you. I have one final question, and I'm not sure it's a concept of a factor that may involve or affect eyewitness identification, but what about time perception? Do people correctly perceive the amount of time an event takes, particularly a stressful event?

A. No. As a matter of fact, people almost invariably overestimate the amount of time that something took. When the event is over and they are now thinking back and trying to provide an accurate estimate of how long it took, classically, they estimate a duration that is too long.

Q. They wouldn't be lying at that point. I mean, they are not intentionally telling an untruth?

A. No, it's an attempt to give an accurate estimate, but it typically is wrong. "Typically" is even too weak a word to use in this case. Most everybody overestimates the amount of time that something took.

Q. And I take it that's been studied?

A. Yes, it has.

Q. And the result reaches is, as you stated, almost always?

A. Yes.

Q. Do you know why? Do psychologists know why?

A. Well, psychologist have tried to find out why by asking questions such as: does it matter whether the interval was filled with activities or whether there were relatively fewer activities in the interval? And they will do an experiment in which they manipulate that factor and, in fact, the answer to that question is yes, it does matter.

Filled intervals are perceived to be longer. So it may be that it has something to do with the fact that many things are happening in the interval and, in a stressful interval, relatively, even more things are happening within the interval. So you do find that even with stressful situations or even with people who are ordinarily stressful/they tend to even more than average overestimate the amount of time that something took.

Appendix 3- Extraneous Information

Mug Shot

Photo Date: 01/20/2000 Photo Time: 09:43 pm

Name: Van Buren, Edward Joseph, Jr. DOB: 08/21/1958

Sex:	M	Hgt:	603	Hair:	BRO
Race:	W	Wgt:	200	Eyes:	BRO
Eth:	N				

Build: M (Medium)
Compl: M (Medium)

SMT:

State Bar of Texas – Disciplinary Actions

2002

On November 7, E. J. Van Buren, Jr. (#20465700), 43 of Houston accepted a public reprimand. The District 4-B Grievance Committee found the complainant hired Van Buren for representation in a criminal matter. Van Buren failed to keep the complainant informed of the status of the case or communicate with the complainant regarding the criminal complaint filed against him. Van Buren violated Rules 1.03(a) and (b).

2003

On June 17, E. J. Van Buren, Jr. [#20465700], 44 of Houston received a four-year, partially probated suspension effective July 1, with the first six months actively served and the remainder probated. The District 4-B Grievance Committee found that on Dec.16, 1999, Van Buren failed to appear before the district court of Montgomery County to conduct a plea for his client. That was Van Buren's ninth failure to appear in that particular case. Van Buren was ordered to serve 30 days in jail for contempt of court. The court appointed another attorney to represent the client, because the client would have had to remain in jail for another 30 days before the client's probation plea could have been processed.

A reporter from the Conroe Courier contacted Van Buren, and according to the reporter Van Buren screamed obscenities about the court and lambasted the judge, calling him, “a bold-faced liar." A story about the matter appeared on the front page of the Courier on Dec.19, 1999. Van Buren violated Rules 1.01(b)(1) and 8.02(a).

2004

On Oct. 27, E. J. Van Buren, Jr. [#20465700], 45 of Houston was disbarred. The 164th District Court of Harris County found Van Buren violated Rules 1.01(b)(1), 1.04(a), 1.14(b), 1.15(d), 8.01(b), and 8.04(a)(3), (a)(8), (a)(11), and (a)(12). He was ordered to pay $9,350 in restitution, $8,000 in attorney's fees, and $367 in cost, plus post-judgment interest of five percent per year.

Judge Bob Burdette

RAILROADED

The Bench Warmer
After two defeats by voters, will Bob Burdette finally lose his black robe to a DWI?
By Tim Fleck
Published on April 12, 2001
www.houstonpress.com

On a Friday even early last month, retired barber Patti Lyn Simon and a friend were driving home after a quiet dinner at Baba Yega in the Montrose area. Simon, a Houston native who is disabled with arthritis of the neck and back, braked her black Nissan pickup at the red light at Montrose and Westheimer. Without warning, an impact racked the 56-year old woman, "like a lightning bolt going through my spine."

Simon's truck had been rear-ended by a green Jaguar driven by Bob Burdette, the 58-year-old Democratic judge who had twice been ousted by voters, only to return as a visiting judge over the protest of then-district attorney Johnny Holmes.

Simon looked back after the collision but could see nothing. Burdette already had piloted his damaged auto to the right and started to turn north on Montrose. Simon's companion, Josephine Boardman, jumped out and caught up to the Jaguar. She pounded on the windows, but Burdette continued turning and nearly hit another vehicle. A couple got out of that car and helped stop him from leaving.

Simon says her arms had gone numb but she angrily asked the driver, "What is wrong with you?"

According to Simon, the tottering man put his arms on her and replied, "I'm drunk."

"This man was so polluted," recalls Simon, "he could barely stand up."

When asked for his license and insurance, the driver produced a business card that read, "Harris County Visiting Judge." He was saying, "I've got to go home now."

Boardman grabbed the judge's keys from the ignition, noting that the car's interior smelled like a distillery.

Police arrest and jailed the judge on misdemeanor charges of driving while intoxicated and failing to stop and give information at an accident. He refused to submit to a Breathalyzer.

An ambulance took Simon to the Taub Hospital. She remained there until the following morning, receiving treatment for back pain.

"I got out an hour and a half before he got out of jail," she chuckles.

Asked for his version of what happened, Burdette declined comment; he is scheduled to appear in court later this month for a preliminary hearing. Lyn McClellan, the district attorney's misdemeanor chief, told the Houston chronicle he wanted guilty pleas on both charges in exchanged for Burdette serving a year's probation and 100 days of community service. Upon reflection, McClellan later declined to discuss any plea offer, saying it might prejudice a jury should the case go to trial.

A courthouse source questions why Burdette wasn't charged under a felony law against drunk drivers who case serious injuries in crashes. Simon is continuing therapy for the effects of the collision, but she agrees with McClellan that then injuries did not warrant a felony charge.

Burdette's attorney Robert C. Bennet declined to reveal if there has been a plea agreement. However, the lawyer dryly observers that, "I don't think you ought to be figuring on covering a long trial."

With the DWI likely to be an open-and-shut case, the real issue is whether Burdette will be allowed to continue as a visiting judge. He has presided over primarily capital murder trials in the county's "project" courts since 1994.

Death row cases require extensive jury selection and trial time, and the project courts were created to process them quickly, freeing up regular judges to handle normal docket duties. Occasionally district judges will take high-profile capital cases, using visiting judges to process the normal flow of cases in their courts.

Burdette was appointed by then-governor Mark White to the 337th District Court bench in 1983.A Republican landslide swept him out of office in 1984, and White came to the rescue in 1986 with an appointment to the 184th court. Eight years later Republican Jan Crocker defeated Burdette, and he went to the newly created project courts.

As district attorney, Holmes opposed the hiring of defeated judges, contending it made a mockery of the electoral system by thwarting the will of the voters. Holmes took his argument to the Texas Court of Criminal Appeals and lost.

Asked about his judicial future, Burdette responded that, "I just want to get this whole thing over with and then just step back and take a look." Burdette says there are no rules that would prohibit his continued services, but the decision is not up to him.

Visiting judges are certified by regional administrative jurist Olen Underwood of Conroe. Bennett would say only that Burdette discussed the situation with Underwood, who did not return an Insider call for comment.

Even if Underwood keeps Burdette on the visiting judges' roster, he would fill in only at the specific invitation of individual judges. That shouldn't be a problem for Burdette, who has plenty of friends among the courthouse judiciary who will likely continue to give him cases if he's available.

"The institution has its own standards," says veteran attorney David A. Jones."As it applies to Burdette, it's called speed in all things. Dispose of cases, dispose of people, and you're okay with them."

Night view of the back half of the Carrington Club parking lot with the area of the shooting labeled.

Close up night view of tire shop and area of Larry Risher's vehicle.

Night view of back half of club's parking lot.

Night view of parking lot in area of shooting with spent shell casings.

Wide night view of back half of club parking lot.

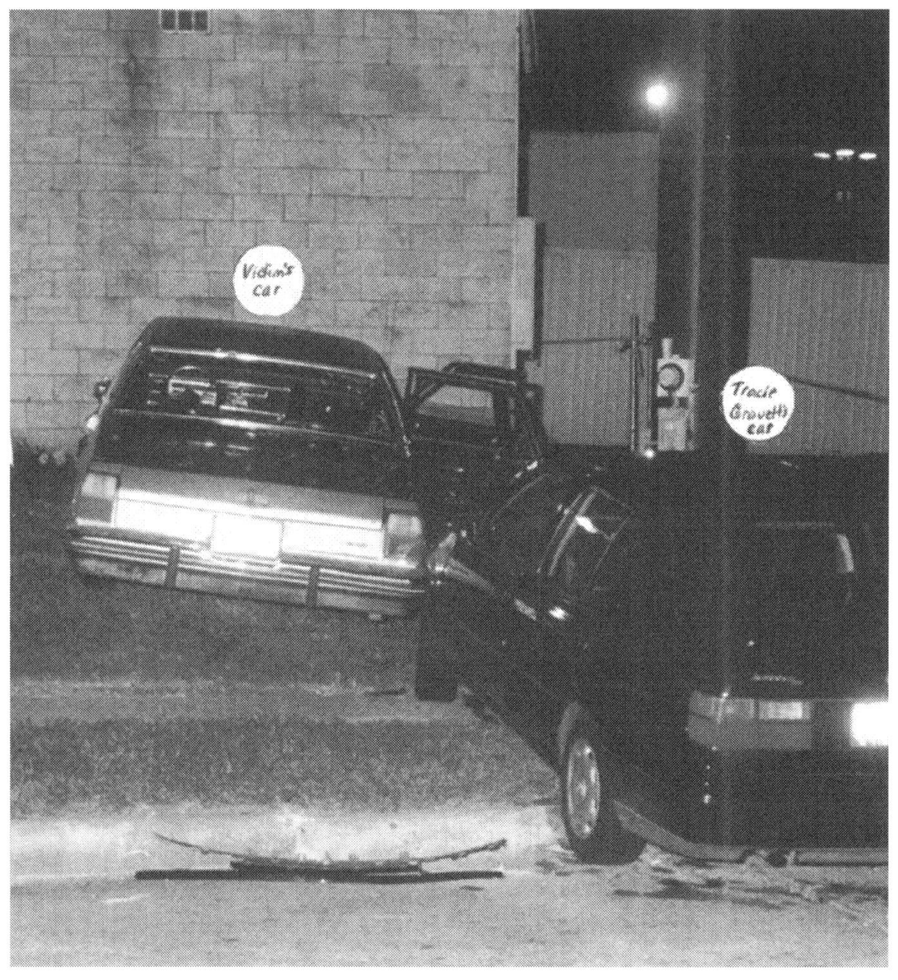

Victim's car after it crashed into Tracie Gravett's car and came to rest beside the Stop N Go.

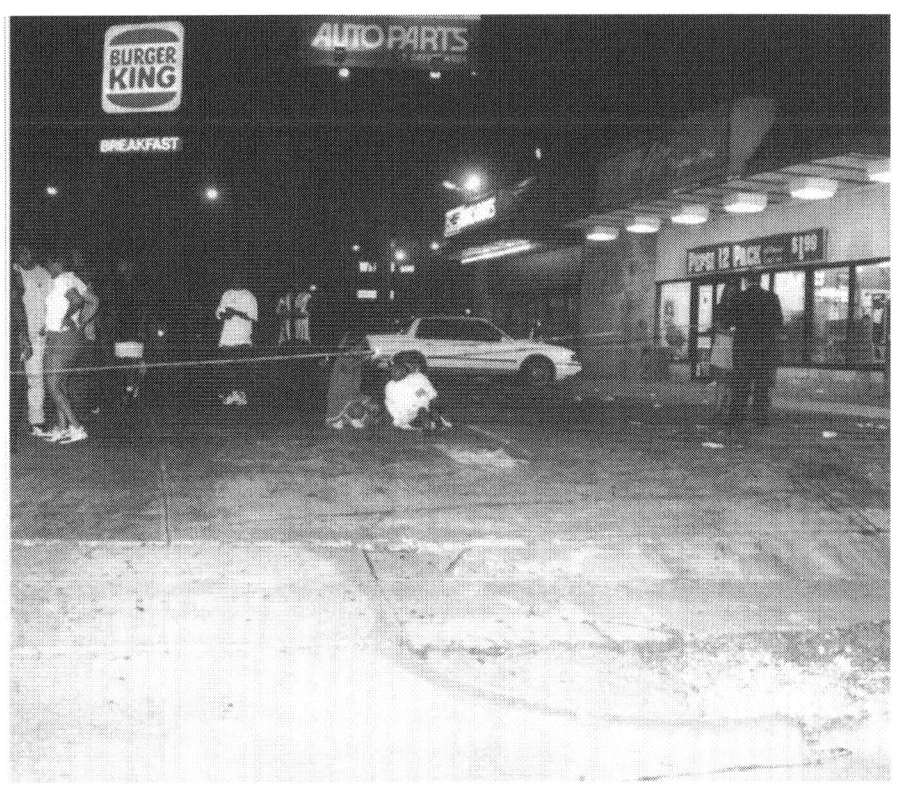

Witness in front of the Stop N Go that remained at the scene after the shooting.

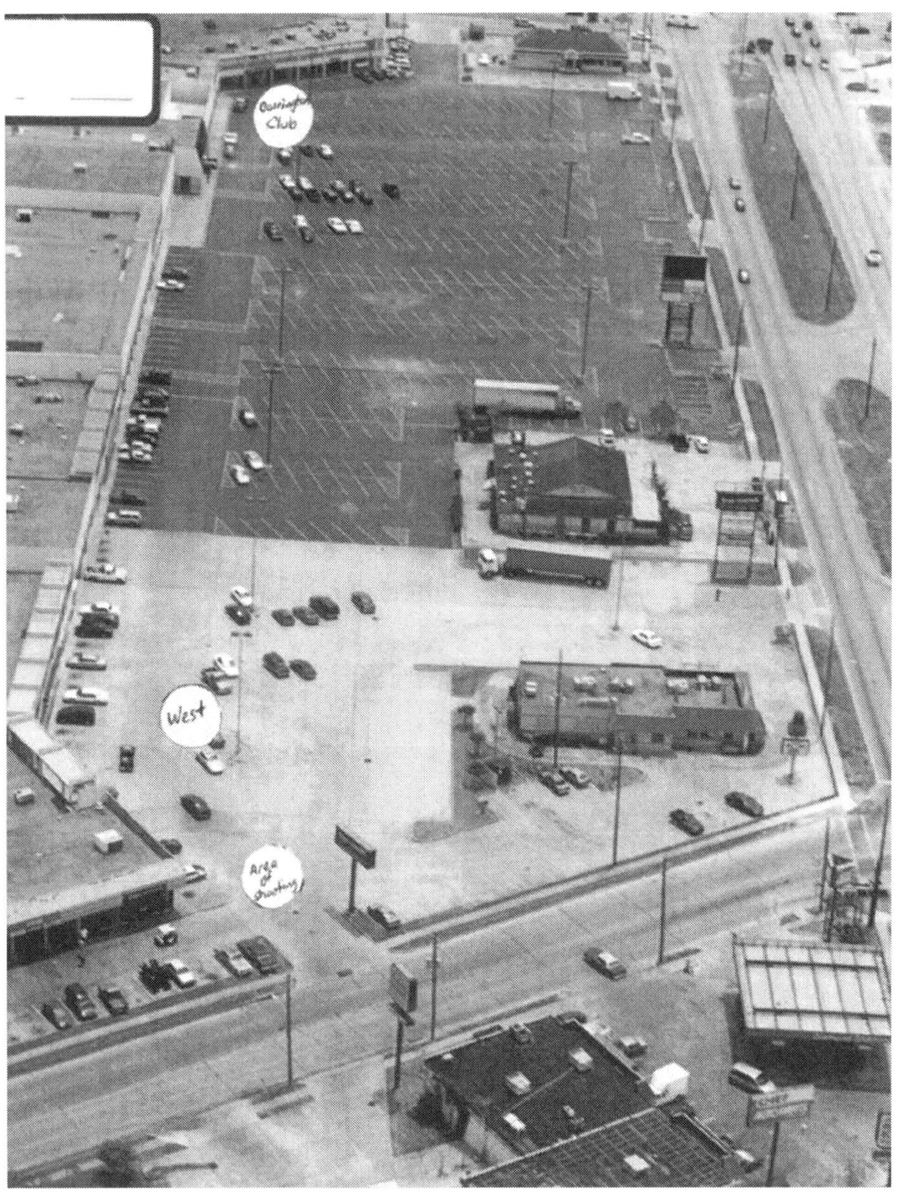

Arial view of the Carrington Club's parking lot with the area of the shooting and location of the Defendant labeled.

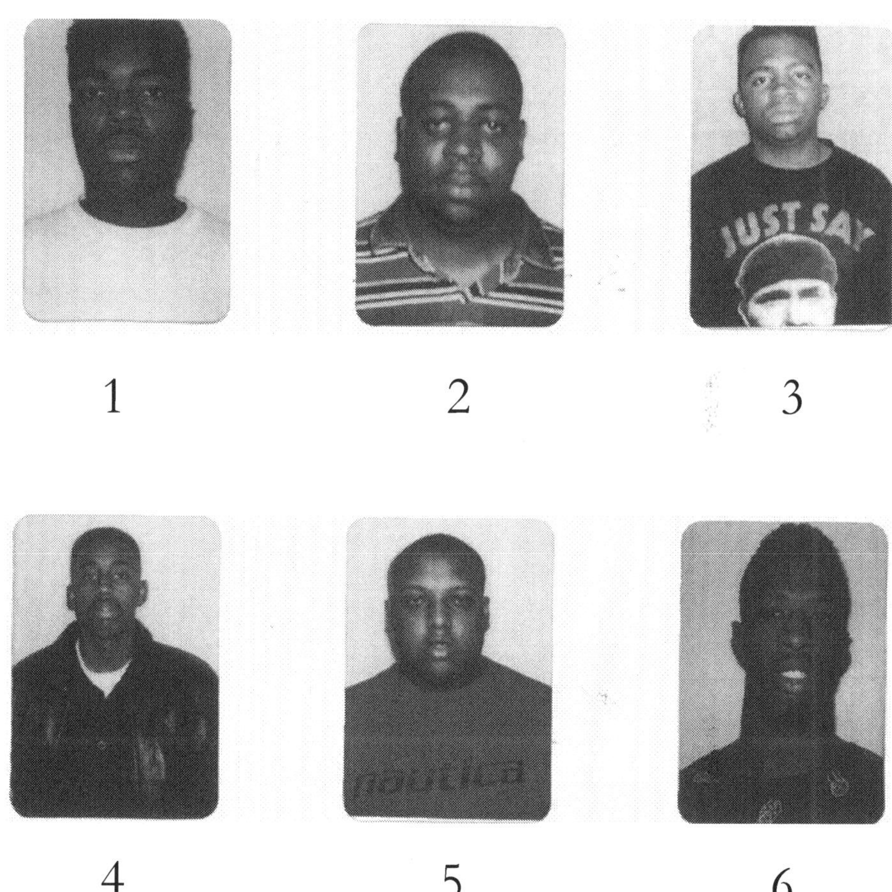

A copy of the photo spread of the Defendant and his Co-Defendant shown to Jerome Sampson and Lawrence Fields on June 12, 1997, six days after the shooting. The Defendant is in the #5 position; the Co-Defendant is in the #2 position.

Appendix 5- An Interview With Kenneth West

D.R: How's it going?

K.W: Pretty good.

D.R: You've been incarcerated for thirteen years now, that's a long time. What have you been up to?

K.W: Besides fighting my cases I've been educating myself. This my first time in prison, I don't want to ever come back.

D.R: That's understandable. How about your appeals? How has that gone?

K.W: I'm still here; so, not too good. But the appeals court in Texas are real conservative, they hate overturning convictions. I think they invented the idea of harmless error.

D.R: Do you believe your appeals had merit?

K.W: Besides being innocent?

D.R: How has being incarcerated affected your family?

K.W: I was engaged to be married when I was first convicted, that didn't happen, and I've had to watch my daughters grow up from the visiting room.

D.R: You currently hold a bachelor's degree?

K.W: No. I still lack five classes to complete my B.S in Sociology with Sam Houston. Right now, I have 3 associates' degrees.

D.R: I know that in this day and age wrongful convictions are a reality. The spate of DNA exonerations proves that much, 250 by last count. But every time I see another innocent man being freed for a crime he didn't commit, usually after he has served decades in prison. The question that's always pops in my mind is out of all people why did that happen to that particular person? Do you understand what I'm asking?

K.W: I do, not a day goes by that I don't try to answer that. The best I've come up with is that I wasn't in a good space, or where I needed to be as a human being. Being young and misguided sometimes you work to create an image and then that image turns around and bites you in the butt. Having authority issues also played a part.

D.R: What do you mean by authority issues?

K.W: Growing up I always saw the police as the enemy. And I never wanted anything to do with them. Yet once I became a suspect the worst thing I could've did was take this attitude into my dealings with the detectives working these cases. The very people in charge of determining which pieces fit where. A respectful, cooperative guy might get the benefit of the doubt, but an arrogant, obnoxious...

D.R: Had you never been involved in the self-defense shooting do you believe you would've been charged let alone convicted of the other shooting in which you weren't involved?

K.W: Absolutely not. Fact is, it's easier to convict a person who snatches a purse on Monday, of another purse snatching on Tuesday; doesn't matter if he did it or not. Logic says, "Well, he did it Monday." Snap judgments like that or second nature to us, it's how we live our lives, and jurors are human. That's what happened to Michael Blair; luckily, DNA was available to prove he didn't do it.

D.R: Maybe this question isn't worth asking, but what, if anything, would you have done differently?

K.W: Besides not being a club rat, and never going near the Carrington's club, I wouldn't have gone to trial.

D.R: But how else could you prove that you're innocent?

K.W: That's the thing, you can't; especially not if you're young, black and poor. You're not going to win; innocent or not. Maybe if you're Robert Durst or Robert Angelton or some other white multi-millionaire, you've got a fair chance. If not, you're going to be found guilty. There's a reason 90% of cases end in plea bargains. The average young African American doesn't stand a chance at a jury trial. I'm so convinced of this from my own and other's experience that I witnessed, that I believe any defense attorney that advises such a client to go to trial in Harris County is irresponsible if not outright ineffective. And conviction rates support this.

D.R: Now that a book has been written about your case, what, if anything, do you hope it accomplishes?

K.W: First I just want the truth to be out there for people to know what's really going on in Harris County. Young black men are being lynched and I was one of them. Injustice thrives on silence; the silence of the nameless and faceless. I studied the history of Germany, because I wanted to know how one man could convince people to murder six million Jews. What I found was because society viewed the Jews as nobodies. Nobody cared. That's the way majority of people in society view us; as nobodies. If we don't yet a fair trial; oh well. Shaky evidence used to convict us; oh well. Represented by ineffective, disbarred lawyers; oh well. That was the same thing the Germany people said when Hitler and his goons started rounding up the Jews; oh well!

D.R: How do you keep your spirits up and from getting involved in all the negative things in the prison environment?

K.W. My faith helps me, along with my desire to move forward, and not backwards. But it's tough to stay positive and keep the faith. Every day is a struggle.

D.R: Do you believe you'll ever yet out of prison?

K.W: I do; one day the truth will come out.

D.R: When that day comes what are your plans?

K.W: (Laughs) Let me see? Get married, and if I'm not too ancient, have some more kids. I would also like to own my own business and to work with at risk youth.

D.R: I wish you luck.

K.W: Thanks.

Made in the USA
Monee, IL
10 December 2021

84686718R00136